Early Learning and Child Well-being

A STUDY OF FIVE-YEAR-OLDS IN ENGLAND, ESTONIA, AND THE UNITED STATES

This work is published under the responsibility of the Secretary-General of the OECD. The opinions expressed and arguments employed herein do not necessarily reflect the official views of OECD member countries.

This document, as well as any data and map included herein, are without prejudice to the status of or sovereignty over any territory, to the delimitation of international frontiers and boundaries and to the name of any territory, city or area.

The statistical data for Israel are supplied by and under the responsibility of the relevant Israeli authorities. The use of such data by the OECD is without prejudice to the status of the Golan Heights, East Jerusalem and Israeli settlements in the West Bank under the terms of international law.

Note by Turkey
The information in this document with reference to "Cyprus" relates to the southern part of the Island. There is no single authority representing both Turkish and Greek Cypriot people on the Island. Turkey recognises the Turkish Republic of Northern Cyprus (TRNC). Until a lasting and equitable solution is found within the context of the United Nations, Turkey shall preserve its position concerning the "Cyprus issue".

Note by all the European Union Member States of the OECD and the European Union
The Republic of Cyprus is recognised by all members of the United Nations with the exception of Turkey. The information in this document relates to the area under the effective control of the Government of the Republic of Cyprus.

Please cite this publication as:
OECD (2020), *Early Learning and Child Well-being: A Study of Five-year-Olds in England, Estonia, and the United States*, OECD Publishing, Paris, *https://doi.org/10.1787/3990407f-en*.

ISBN 978-92-64-51930-5 (print)
ISBN 978-92-64-48086-5 (pdf)

Foreword

It is not always easy for policy makers to make decisions in education that are focused on the future, on what our children need from education. It is easier to rely on what worked in the past, at least for some children, than to continuously question and try to understand how children are really faring. Yet making decisions in the absence of robust evidence is risky.

Many countries have increased their focus on early childhood education and care, with an expectation that children's outcomes would be subsequently improved in school and beyond. Participation rates in early childhood education have increased, greater attention is being given to early years' curricula and pedagogy, and more early childhood educators have advanced qualifications than ever before. The benefits for children, however, are not always apparent. At the same time, the international evidence countries can draw on to inform their policy approaches for children's early learning is sparse.

The three countries that participated in the International Early Learning and Child Well-being Study - England (United Kingdom), Estonia and the United States - wished to better understand how well five-year-old children in their country were faring, in relation to children in other countries. These countries wished to create a common basis for countries to learn from each other on how to improve children's early learning and well-being. They also wished to have a means to benchmark their progress over time.

The study investigated how well five-year-old children were developing across the range of early skills they need to succeed in education and grow up into happy, healthy and responsible citizens. These skills include both early cognitive development and social-emotional development. Children without this balance of skills will struggle to do well in school and in other areas of their lives. The study includes a direct assessment of children's development and skills, enabling children to show us how they are really doing.

The study highlights early differences between children, such as between boys and girls and between children from advantaged and disadvantaged families. This helps us to see how we can better support children and their families, both in the earliest years and in the first years of schooling. Education systems that orient their priorities from an institutional lens to children's actual needs will have greater success overall and will be better able to achieve improved equity.

Children love to learn and supportive, caring environments help them to do so. Our job is to ensure we are providing such environments.

Andreas Schleicher
Director for the Directorate for Education and Skills
Special Advisor on Education Policy to the Secretary General

Acknowledgements

The International Early Learning and Child Well-being Study (IELS) was a collaborative effort between participating countries and the OECD secretariat.

The development of this report was guided by Andreas Schleicher and Yuri Belfali. The lead author of the report was Rowena Phair, with chapters contributed by Javier Suarez-Alvarez (Chapter 4), Malek Abu-Jawdeh (Chapter 5) and Lauren Kavanagh (Chapter 6). The publication was edited by Sally Hinchcliffe and designed by Fung Kwan Tam. Administrative support was provided by Valentine Bekka and Matthew Gill. Communications support was provided by Rachel Linden.

To support the technical implementation of IELS, the OECD contracted an international consortium of institutions, led by Maurice Walker at the Australian Council for Educational Research (ACER). The consortium included the International Association for the Evaluation of Educational Achievement (IEA), led by Anja Waschk, and cApStAn, under the lead of Roberta Lizzi.

To help to ensure that the study was rigorous and valid, IELS was guided and supported in its work by a Technical Advisory Group (TAG) and a Measurement Advisory Group (MAG). The members of the TAG were Iram Siraj (Chair), Rosemary Cahill, and Szilvia Papp. The members of the MAG were Ray Adams, Alla Berezner, Dan Cloney, Wolfram Schulz, Maurice Walker, and Nathan Zoanetti. Both groups provided input to the assessment framework for the study, instrument development for the assessments and contextual information, and the analysis of the findings.

This volume was prepared in close collaboration with the IELS teams from England, Estonia and the United States, led by Frances Forsyth, Tiina Peterson and Mary Coleman respectively. Their input to this report is gratefully acknowledged.

Table of contents

BOXES

FIGURES

TABLES

Follow OECD Publications on:

http://twitter.com/OECD_Pubs

http://www.facebook.com/OECDPublications

http://www.linkedin.com/groups/OECD-Publications-4645871

http://www.youtube.com/oecdilibrary

http://www.oecd.org/oecddirect/

This book has...

StatLinks

A service that delivers Excel® files from the printed page!

Look for the *StatLinks* at the bottom of the tables or graphs in this book. To download the matching Excel® spreadsheet, just type the link into your Internet browser, starting with the *http://dx.doi.org* prefix, or click on the link from the e-book edition.

Executive Summary

Starting behind in the early years means staying behind – for individual children and for an education system as a whole. A child's development in the first few years of life significantly predicts his or her later success in education and ongoing levels of happiness and well-being. The most effective investment governments can make to enhance education and later life outcomes is to provide a strong start in children's early years. Seeking to ameliorate individual or systemic learning issues at later ages is less successful and more costly than doing so earlier.

Education systems that wish to achieve a step-change in student outcomes are well advised to increase their focus on the quality, responsiveness and effectiveness of their early years policies for children. Like all areas of education policy, decisions affecting children's early years of learning and well-being are fraught with political and commercial interests, in addition to ideology. Many claim they know what is best for children, yet the international data in this field is surprisingly limited. Moreover, while children's needs and interests have always been diverse, children's lives are changing at a greater pace than ever before. Thus, research findings on how best to support children and their families from 20, 10 or even 5 years ago may not be fully applicable to today's youngsters.

The International Early Learning and Child Well-being study puts a spotlight on how children are faring at five years of age. The study directly measures key indicators of children's development and learning, as well as collecting a broad range of developmental and contextual information from children's parents and teachers. The study does not measure everything. Instead, it focuses on those aspects of development and learning that are predictive of children's later education outcomes and wider well-being. These are: emergent literacy[1] and emergent numeracy[2], self-regulation[3], and social-emotional skills[4]. Across these early learning domains, a total of 10 dimensions of children's development and learning were included in the study.

Three OECD countries participated in this study: England (United Kingdom), Estonia and the United States. Each of these countries recognises children's early years as critical to children's later learning and well-being. Each country participated in this study to enhance the body of international evidence available to policy makers, education leaders, practitioners and parents to improve children's early learning outcomes. The information from the study provides each country with insights to inform their approaches to children's early years and their approaches in the early years of schooling. At five years of age, there is much that education systems can do to further support the learning trajectories for these children.

EARLY DIFFERENCES BETWEEN COUNTRIES AND GROUPS OF CHILDREN ARE CLEARLY EVIDENT

The study found clear differences in children's early learning across the three countries. Five-year-olds in Estonia demonstrated a well-rounded balance of skills, with strengths in emergent literacy, self-regulation and social-emotional skills. In particular, children in Estonia were more able to recognise the emotions of others, a precursor for empathy, and were reported by their teachers as having higher prosocial skills than children in England or the United States.

Children in England demonstrated stronger skills in emergent numeracy than children in either Estonia or the United States. The findings in England for emergent literacy, working memory and mental flexibility were similar to those in Estonia. Teachers in England - and in the United States - reported five-year-olds as less disruptive than reported by teachers in Estonia.

Additionally, children in the United States were found to have similar levels in inhibiting impulses and in trusting others to children in Estonia. The emergent literacy and emergent numeracy skills of children in the United States, however, were significantly lower than for children in Estonia and England. This gap was particularly pronounced in emergent numeracy, consistent with the relatively lower levels of mathematics competencies found in 15-year-olds in the United States in the OECD's Programme for international Student Assessment (PISA).

Gender differences were found in all three countries. Girls had stronger emergent literacy and higher levels of social-emotional skills than boys in each country. Girls were better able to identify others' emotions and reports from parents and teachers identified girls as having higher prosocial skills and to be less disruptive than boys. The direct assessment found no discernible differences between girls and boys in emergent numeracy, although girls were reported by their parents and teachers as having higher levels of emergent numeracy than boys. Overall, girls demonstrated slightly stronger skills than boys in the direct assessment of self-regulation but again, parent and teacher reports for girls were more positive than for boys.

Differences in children's skills were also found in relation to the child's socio-economic background, consistent with other international studies. Children from high socio-economic backgrounds had higher levels of skills than children from low socio-economic backgrounds across almost all learning domains in the study. Estonia had the smallest differences amongst children based on their socio-economic backgrounds whereas the greatest differences were found in the United States.

WHAT PARENTS DO IS PIVOTAL FOR THEIR CHILDREN'S DEVELOPMENT

The day-to-day activities that parents undertake are highly correlated with children's learning and development. Regardless of socio-economic background, the study found children did better when their parents

- Read to them almost every day

- Ensured there were many children's books in the home

- Had back-and-forth conversations with them

- Took them to special activities such as dance, swimming or scouts

- Were involved in the ECEC centre or school they attend.

At the same time, the study found that moderate engagement in most activities was more strongly associated with children's learning than daily frequency. For example, children who attended special activities three or four times a week had higher scores than children who attended such activities every day. An exception was reading, where the findings show that reading five to seven days a week with children was more strongly correlated with children's emergent literacy and their social-emotional skills than reading to them less frequently. Nonetheless, reading to children three to four times a week was still associated with stronger skill development than reading to children once a week or not at all.

EARLY CHILDHOOD EDUCATION AND CARE ALSO MAKES A POSITIVE DIFFERENCE

Almost all children in England and Estonia attend some form of early childhood education and care (ECEC) setting by the age of three. In the United States, 51% of children in this study had attended ECEC by the age of three years or younger, although children from high socio-economic families had higher participation rates.

Children in the United States who had attended ECEC demonstrated higher emergent literacy skills and much higher emergent numeracy skills than children who had never attended ECEC, regardless of their socio-economic background. Attending ECEC was not, however, significantly associated with children's self-regulation or social-emotional skills in either a positive or negative direction. IELS found no discernible benefits from starting ECEC before three years of age.

MOST FIVE-YEAR-OLDS USE ELECTRONIC DEVICES

Most of the five-year-olds in the study (83%) used a digital device at least once a week and 42% did so on a daily basis.

There were no clear relationships between the regular use of electronic devices and children's development and skills. There was, however, a positive relationship between the frequency of device use and the mental flexibility skills of children in Estonia and the United States but this was not the case in England. There were also some positive associations between device use and emergent literacy in England and the United States, but not in Estonia.

CHILDREN'S LEARNING IS INTER-RELATED AND MUTUALLY REINFORCING

There were positive relationships between each of the 10 dimensions of children's early development and learning in this study. Emergent literacy and emergent numeracy were strongly correlated, and these also correlated positively with self-regulation skills, particularly mental flexibility and working memory. At the same time, there were positive associations between the cognitive aspects of the study (emergent literacy, emergent numeracy and self-regulation) and children's social-emotional skills, particularly with empathy and prosocial behaviour. Thus, children's learning gains in any one area support ongoing development in other areas of their development.

Notes

1. Emergent literacy refers to the skills children develop that are a precursor to literacy and enable them to understand and communicate with others. In this study, there was no assessment of whether children could read or write.

2. Emergent numeracy refers to simple problem solving and the application of concepts and reasoning in relation to numbers and counting, working with numbers, shape and space, measurement and pattern

3. Self-regulation refers to the skills children develop to inhibit their impulses and direct their thought processes, enabling them to concentrate, retain information and complete short tasks.

4. Social-emotional skills refer to children's abilities in interacting well with others and in managing their emotions.

Reader's guide

WHAT IS IELS?

The International Early Learning and Child Well-being Study (IELS) puts a spotlight on how children are faring at five years of age. IELS directly measures key indicators of children's learning, as well as collecting a broad range of development and contextual information from children's parents and teachers.

WHAT ASPECTS OF LEARNING AND DEVELOPMENT WERE OF FOCUS IN IELS?

IELS conceptualises early earning as holistic, involving cognitive and social-emotional skills whose development are interrelated and mutually reinforcing. The study does not measure everything. Instead, it focuses on those aspects of development and learning that are predictive of children's later education outcomes and wider well-being. These are: emergent literacy and emergent numeracy, self-regulation, and social-emotional skills. Across these main early learning domains, 10 dimensions of children's development and learning were included in the study.

WHO PARTICIPATED IN IELS?

Three OECD countries participated in the study: England (United Kingdom), Estonia and the United States. This report uses "England" as shorthand for England (United Kingdom). IELS covered children who were aged between five and six years during the study administration period of October to December 2018 and who were enrolled in a registered school or early childhood education centre. Samples were drawn and weighted to be representative of the target populations in each of the three participating countries. This report uses "five-year-olds" as shorthand for the IELS target population.

Parents and teachers also participated in IELS by providing contextual information about children's learning and lives. "Teachers" is the term used to describe the teachers or early childhood education and care (ECEC) staff members who responded to teacher questionnaires in IELS. The report uses "parents" as shorthand for the parents, guardians or others who completed the IELS parent questionnaire with respect to participating children.

WHAT DOES THIS VOLUME CONTAIN?

The results from IELS are presented in four reports: an international report and an in-depth report on each of the three participating countries. This international report focuses on the aggregate findings from all three countries.

A GUIDE TO INTERPRETING FINDINGS IN THIS REPORT

Data underlying the report

IELS results are based on direct and indirect assessment of children's skills in a range of learning domains. IELS scores are not physical units (such as meters or grams). Instead, they are set in relation to the variation in outcomes observed across all children who participated. The metric for all learning scales in IELS is the same. There is theoretically no minimum or maximum score in IELS; rather, the data are scaled to have approximately normal distributions, with the means around 500 and standard deviations around 100. A one-point difference on the IELS scale therefore corresponds to an effect size of .01 of a standard deviation and a 10-point difference to an effect size of .1. Results are presented for a subgroup of children only when estimates are based on at least 30 children from at least five ECEC centres or schools.

Important contextual information about children's lives and learning was collected from their parents and teachers. Some information was collected only from teachers, some only from parents, and in some cases, parents and teachers both provided perspectives on the same issue (e.g. how well a child is developing in a particular domain). When parent and teacher reports are compared in tables or figures in this report, those analyses are based on the subsample of children for whom both parents and teachers provided information.

Overall IELS averages

Where cross-country averages are provided in any of the IELS volumes, these averages correspond to the arithmetic mean of the three country estimates.

Statistically significant differences

Unless otherwise stated, a difference reported as statistically significant is significant at the .05 level. This means there is a less than 5% probability that the reported difference occurred by chance; a statistical test has been carried out to establish this. Statistically significant differences in this report are denoted by darker tones in figures and by bold font in tables.

Interpreting correlations

A correlation coefficient is a measure of the degree to which two variables tend to move together. The coefficient has a value between plus and minus 1, which indicates the strength and direction of association. If a correlation is positive, it means that as one variable increases, so does the other. If a correlation is negative, it means that as one variable increases, the other decreases. In this report, a correlation coefficient with an absolute value between 0 and 0.19 is interpreted as weak, between 0.20 and 0.49 as moderate, between .50 and 0.79 as strong, and between 0.80 and .99 as very strong.

Standard deviation

The standard deviation is a measure of the dispersion of a set of data from its mean. The more spread apart the data, the higher the deviation. In a normal distribution, 68% of the scores are within one standard deviation of the mean, 95% within two standard deviations, and 99% within three. As mentioned above, IELS learning scales all have an approximate standard deviation of 100.

Standard error

Scores reported in this volume are population estimates, based on the sample of children selected. However, it is unlikely that the 'true' or population mean is exactly the same as the sample. Some variation or error around estimates is to be expected. Thus, each mean has a standard error, which allows us to estimate how accurately the mean found in our sample reflects the 'true' mean in the population. The 'true' mean score can be found in an interval that is 1.96 standard errors on either side of the obtained mean, 95% of the time.

Rounding figures

As a result of rounding, some figures in tables may not add up exactly to the totals. Totals, averages and differences are calculated on the basis of exact numbers and are rounded only after calculation. Percentages and mean scores are rounded to whole numbers, and standard errors are rounded to two decimal places.

Additional technical information

Readers interested in additional technical detail regarding IELS are directed towards the short technical note at the end of this volume and to the IELS Technical Report (OECD, 2020).

This report uses the OECD StatLinks service, meaning that all tables and figures are assigned a URL leading to an Excel workbook containing the underlying data. These URLs are stable and will remain unchanged over time. In addition, readers of the e-books will be able to click directly on these links, and the workbook will open in a separate window if their Internet browser is open and running.

Abbreviations and acronyms

ACER	Australian Council for Educational Research
CPC	Chicago Child-Parent Center Program
ECEC	Early childhood education and care
EPPE	Effective Pre-school and Primary Education Project
GDP	Gross domestic product
IEA	International Association for the Evaluation of Educational Achievement
IELS	International Early Learning and Child Well-being Study
ISCED	International Standard Classification of Education
PISA	Programme for International Student Assessment
SDG	Sustainable Development Goal
SES	Socio-economic status

Why early learning and child well-being matter

The International Early Learning and Child Well-Being Study (IELS) puts a spotlight on how children are faring at age five. This chapter presents the rationale for focusing on children's learning and development in the earliest years, and outlines the importance of having evidence on early learning that is comparable across countries.

THE EARLY YEARS: A WINDOW OF OPPORTUNITY … AND RISK

The first five years of every child's life are a period of great opportunity, but also one of risk. The cognitive and social-emotional skills that children develop in these early years have long-lasting impacts on their later outcomes throughout schooling and adulthood. While the quality of schooling also matters, strong early learning accelerates later development whereas a poor start inhibits it.

Early learning and children's well-being are inter-related and mutually reinforcing. Children thrive in caring families, where they feel safe and happy, and where they are supported as they learn about themselves and their social, cultural and physical environments. The day-to-day interactions and activities between young children and their parents and other family members foster their well-being and their emerging cognitive and social-emotional skills.

Children also learn in settings beyond their immediate home, including in their wider family network, their neighbourhood community, in early childhood education and care (ECEC) settings and in school. ECEC can be beneficial for all children. For children without strong home learning environments, however, ECEC and early schooling may be their only chance to develop the key skills they need. Children from even the most impoverished homes thrive when they have sustained access to high-quality and responsive learning environments. This early platform of learning enables them to develop the skills to succeed at school and in later life.

The window for positive early learning closes when children are around seven years old, due to a sharp decrease in brain malleability at this point (Stiles and Jernigan, 2010[1]). Protective factors that support children's development during this phase include regular, warm, stimulating interactions with their parents and other caregivers whereas risk factors that impede development include exposure to stresses, such as violence in the home and poor nutrition.

Children who experience supportive early learning environments develop rapidly, establishing a sound base for ongoing learning and achievement. Children who do not have a good start, however, can still be assisted through well-targeted investments that increase the balance of protective factors over risk factors. This enables timely development and shapes children's long-term ability to learn, as illustrated in Figure 1.1.

Figure 1.1 **Risk and protective factors affect development trajectories**

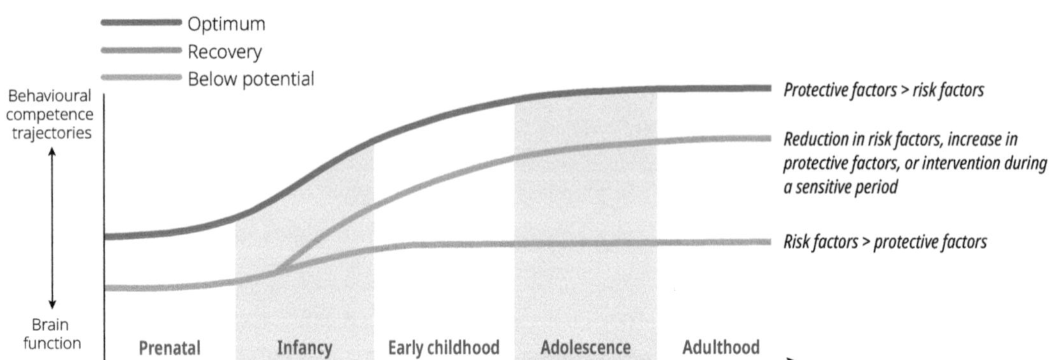

Source: Adapted from Walker et al. (2011[2])Early Childhood Stimulation Benefits Adult Competence and Reduces Violent Behavior, https://doi.org/10.1542/peds.2010-2231.

If children have not developed core foundation skills at seven years of age, they will struggle to progress well at school and are more likely to have social and behavioural difficulties in adolescence and in adulthood. Seeking to ameliorate a poor start at older ages is complex, challenging and costly, with limited success rates (Heckman, 2006[3]). At a system level, the proportion of children who have poor early development constrains the extent to which any education system can achieve success for these children and perform well as a whole.

Countries are increasingly focusing on early years policies, as a means of raising overall educational performance and mitigating disadvantage. Many countries have increased ECEC participation rates and increased their overall investments in early years policies, as shown in Figure 1.2 (OECD, 2019[4]). The expected benefits for children, however, are not always apparent. Despite this, early learning remains one of the most neglected areas of educational research, especially in an international context. As a consequence, there is little international evidence on how to improve early years policies and achieve better results for children.

There could be many reasons why the promise of early childhood education is not delivering for some children. These may include the quality and responsiveness of provision, whether the provision focuses on the skills children need to develop most in the early years, and the timeliness and continuity of provision. At a system level, there is much that countries could learn from each other about how to ensure effective provision for all children.

Figure 1.2 **Change in enrolment rates of children aged 3 to 5 years (2005, 2010 and 2017)**

Early childhood education (ISCED 0) and primary education

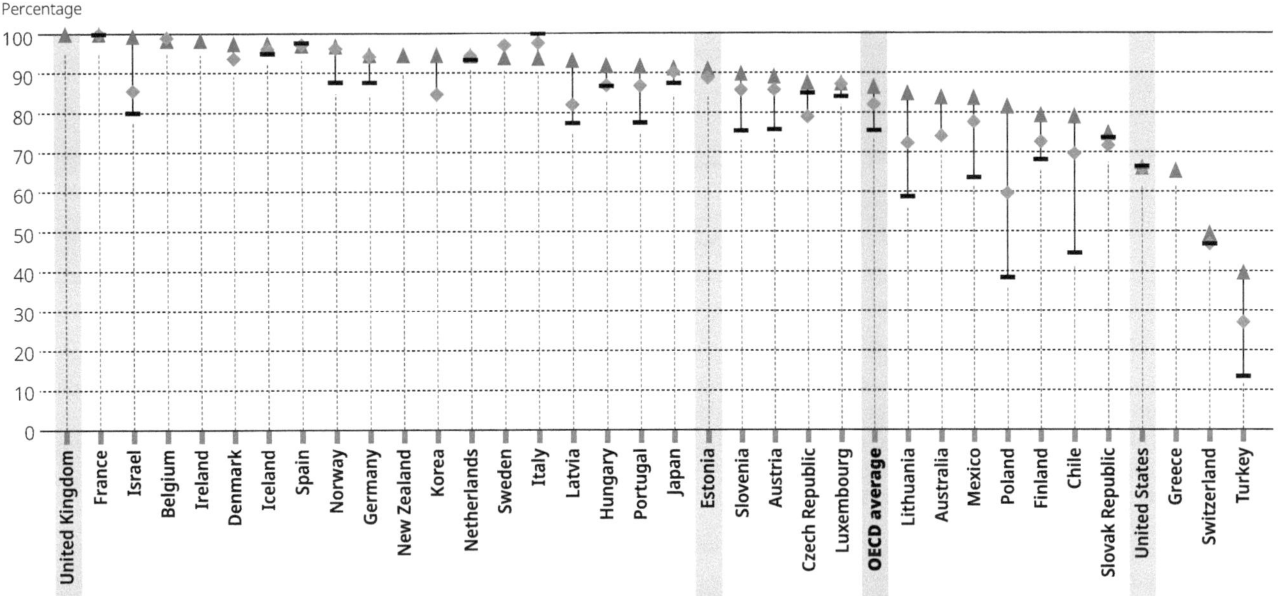

Source: OECD (2019[4]), Education at a Glance *OECD Indicators*, OECD Publishing, Paris, https://dx.doi.org/10.1787/f8d7880d-en.
StatLink https://doi.org/10.1787/888934099979

The remainder of this chapter addresses:

- the impacts of the early years on children's well-being, education and later outcomes
- the areas of learning that matter most for children
- the contexts in which children learn
- the benefits of giving all children a strong early start and the risks of not doing so
- how governments can assess their early years policies.

A STRONG PREDICTOR OF LATER OUTCOMES

Children's early learning and well-being have a direct and enduring impact on their later educational attainment, socio-economic status, health, well-being and civic engagement. An increasing body of longitudinal evidence[1] has tracked children from pre-school and through schooling into adulthood, consistently finding a significant relationship between their early experiences and later outcomes (Shuey and Kankaraš, 2018[5]). The benefits of strong early learning are clearly evident at school entry, at the end of compulsory schooling and later in adulthood. Children who do not develop critical early skills such as emergent literacy or self-regulation, however, face enormous challenges in achieving well at school and in having positive outcomes during adulthood.

An argument against early years investment has been that early skills fadeout in primary school. This is true, yet longitudinal studies demonstrate that the impact of positive early learning re-emerges later in schooling and continues into adulthood, as shown in Figure 1.3. In fact, children's test scores at the age of five better predict adult outcomes than those in primary school. Strong early learning appears to act as a foundation that, once consolidated during early schooling, then provides a protective and fertile base for greater skill development during the remaining school years and into adolescence and adulthood.

Figure 1.3 **Predicted percentage effects on adult earnings of early childhood programmes, based on test scores versus adult outcomes**

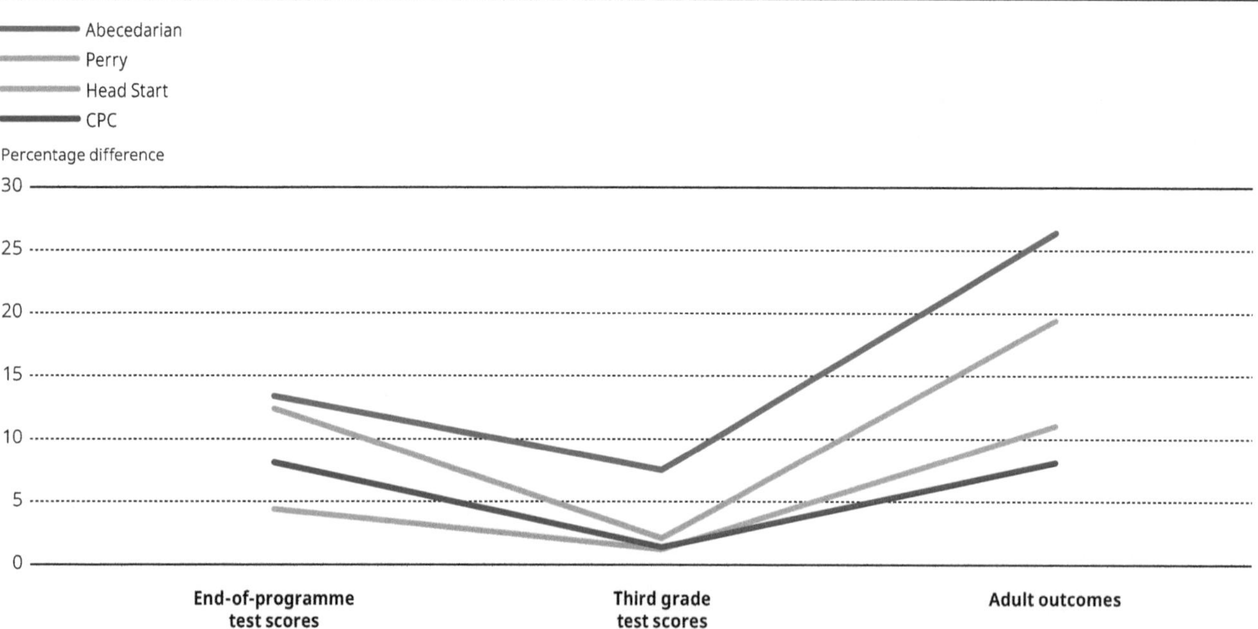

Note: Adult earnings effects are shown as predicted average percentage increase in earnings due to the programme, compared to expected earnings if the person had not participated in the programme. CPC refers to Chicago Child-Parent Center Program.
Source: Bartik (2014[6]), From Preschool to Prosperity: The Economic Payoff to Early Childhood Education, W.E. Upjohn Institute, http://dx.doi.org/10.17848/9780880994835.
StatLink https://doi.org/10.1787/888934110220

Children's early learning and well-being also affect a wide-range of interrelated outcomes in later life. For example, higher educational achievement and attainment are often linked with more positive employment and earnings, as well as with better mental and physical health (OECD, 2018).

The size of early learning effects on adult outcomes is significant. The four longitudinal studies in Figure 1.3 found effect sizes on adult incomes ranging from just under 10% to over 25%.

Early learning supports children's well-being and happiness

There is no trade-off between early learning and children's happiness or indeed from a child's perspective, between learning and play. Happy, healthy children are active and curious, and enjoy the natural processes of learning. These processes occur through interactions with family and other caregivers, and through different types of play. Through these experiences children learn about and actively explore their world, as they also develop their language and other cognitive skills, social-emotional skills, and physical skills (Shuey and Kankaraš, 2018[5]).

As well as developing emergent literacy skills, interactions with others help children learn to express their feelings and preferences, listen to others, share, self-regulate their emotions, solve problems, pay attention and concentrate. Children who develop this holistic set of skills are happier than children who do not have the opportunities to do so. These early skills influence how well children get along with others and how well they are able to make friends. Children's skills also influence the extent to which adults engage with them, further affecting their sense of connectedness and well-being, and their continuing skill development.

Better outcomes throughout schooling

Early academic skills such as emergent literacy and emergent numeracy are positively associated with later educational achievement. Self-regulation, visual-motor skills and agreeableness in early childhood all predict later educational attainment. These early skills are evident in the skills students demonstrate at the end of primary school and at the end of secondary school, including higher rates of school completion (Shuey and Kankaraš, 2018[5]).

Strong early learning translates into higher levels of skills at later ages because "skills beget skills" (Cunha and Heckman, 2009[7]). Early progress enables children to take greater advantage of further learning opportunities inside and outside school than children without such positive foundations. Children with strong early learning outcomes elicit additional learning opportunities from their parents, teachers and environment, by asking questions or taking the initiative to engage in new activities.

Strong early learning also reduces the need for special education support and remedial education during schooling (Sylva et al., 2004[8]; Siraj et al., 2017[9]).

Children with poor emergent literacy skills can appear to do well in the first year or two of school. However, these children understand fewer words per interaction, focus primarily on commands and tend to interact less with adults than children with better language skills. After two years of primary school, children with weaker early literacy skills increasingly struggle, particularly in reading, and often face a downward spiral from this point (Shuey and Kankaraš, 2018[5]).

Early self-regulation is also critical to later educational achievement, even after controlling for early literacy and numeracy skills (Duncan et al., 2007[10]). Aspects of self-regulation such as attentiveness and task persistence among children starting school are positively associated with achievement in reading and mathematics throughout primary school (Li-Grining et al., 2010[11]).

Early self-regulation relates positively to teachers' perceptions of children's abilities (Neuenschwander et al., 2012[12]) and thus their expectations of them. Self-regulation appears to be particularly important for boys (Washbrook, Propper and Sayal, 2013[13]) and for children from low-income or at-risk families in predicting later education outcomes.

Higher educational attainment following school

Early academic skills such as emergent literacy and numeracy are positively associated with educational attainment in adulthood. In addition, self-regulation, agreeableness, visual-motor skills, and prosocial behaviour in early childhood all predict adult educational attainment, such as completing a degree. Both self-regulation and early agreeableness have been found to be associated with higher academic attainment in adulthood, even after adjusting for earlier cognitive ability. Early self-regulation has also been found to be a stronger predictor of degree completion by the age of 25 than early reading or maths scores (McClelland et al., 2013[14]).

In addition to the attainment of degrees and other qualifications, early skills have been found to be predictive of adult literacy and numeracy skills, as indicated by test scores at different ages during adulthood. For example, children's persistence in completing a task as four-year-olds significantly predicted their reading and mathematics test scores at the age of 21 (McClelland et al., 2013[14]).

Stronger employment and socio-economic outcomes

Strong early cognitive skills, self-regulation skills and social well-being have clear positive associations with employment, income and socio-economic status in adulthood. For example, five-year-olds with stronger verbal skills are more likely as adults to be employed, earn a higher income and own their own home (Schoon et al., 2015[15]). Similar associations have been found for early numeracy and visual-motor skills.

Similarly, adults who succeeded in moving out of poverty they experienced as children generally displayed higher cognitive skills in their early years than those from similar circumstances who remained in poverty as adults (Blanden, 2006). Adults who achieved social mobility due to enhanced early learning have been found to pass similar benefits on to their own children (Heckman and Karapukula, 2019[16]).

Early cognitive skills are a stronger predictor of adult earnings for women than for men, although in a negative rather than positive direction. Women who had low early cognitive skills faced larger wage penalties in the labour market than men who had similarly low levels of early cognitive skills (Parsons et al., 2011[17]).

Early self-regulation has also been found to be linked to labour market outcomes. Better early self-regulation is related to a lower likelihood of unemployment, welfare dependence, including social housing, and higher income levels in adulthood (Moffitt et al., 2011[18]; Fergusson, Boden and Horwood, 2013[19]).

In addition, early social competence is associated with better work competence, as well as predicting entrepreneurial status, continuity of entrepreneurial activity and earnings.

Better mental and physical health

Early cognitive skills, self-regulation, emotional health and social skills are all associated with better mental health in adulthood. Children with better receptive language skills as five-year-olds were more likely to have positive mental health outcomes in adulthood, including a lower likelihood of depression, anxiety and psychological distress. Better self-regulation and visual-motor skills at age five are also associated with lower malaise in adulthood. Conversely, poor early self-regulation is associated with later psychological disorders, particularly for men (Schoon et al., 2015[15]).

Early cognitive abilities, self-regulation, visual-motor skills, agreeableness, and conscientiousness are all linked with adult physical health. This includes better self-reported health and better eating habits and lower likelihoods of obesity, smoking and substance abuse (Schoon et al., 2015[15]).

Better citizens

Strong language skills, self-regulation, trust and empathy in early childhood predict a lower likelihood of involvement in crime and delinquency in adulthood. Aspects of social well-being, particularly prosocial behaviours, are also important predictors of a lower likelihood of crime and delinquency later in life.

Conversely, children who demonstrate a lack of empathy and trust during their early years are more likely to demonstrate antisocial and delinquent behaviours later in adolescence, and also face greater risk of adult psychopathology (Fontaine et al., 2011[20]). In particular, poor early self-regulation and a lack of prosocial behaviours are related to violent offending in particular, and the likelihood and number of criminal offences in adulthood (Fergusson, Boden and Horwood, 2013[19]).

THE AREAS OF EARLY LEARNING THAT MATTER MOST FOR CHILDREN

Four areas of children's early learning are critical in predicting later outcomes in schooling and adulthood: emergent literacy, emergent numeracy, self-regulation and social-emotional skills. While these areas overlap, they each have an independent effect on later outcomes. And while other areas of children's development also matter, such as visual-motor and physical skills, the interrelated and overlapping nature of early learning means it is not necessary to measure every skill to have an accurate indication of how well a child is developing.

Figure 1.4 **Key areas of early learning and child well-being**

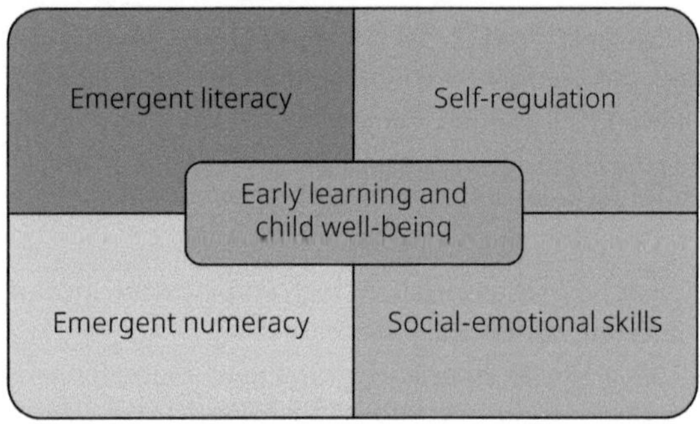

Children who are progressing well in the four areas in Figure 1.4 have a high likelihood of going on to do well at school, realise their aspirations, achieve economic independence and live happy, healthy lives.

Emergent literacy

In the early years, the most important components of emergent literacy are listening comprehension, vocabulary and phonological awareness. These are more predictive of children's later literacy skills than other literacy-related development, such as the level of reading and writing skills that children have developed at the age of five.

Listening comprehension incorporates a range of early literacy skills, such as understanding the explicit and implied meaning of spoken language, including standalone sentences. Vocabulary knowledge is fundamental for comprehension and for successfully communicating with others, which further develops emergent literacy as well as social connectedness. Phonological awareness is the ability to detect, manipulate and analyse the auditory aspects of spoken language.

Self-regulation

Self-regulation refers to the mental processes that enable individuals to plan, focus their attention, remember instructions and juggle multiple tasks successfully. The key elements of self-regulation that predict children's later outcomes are referred to as executive function. This includes working memory, inhibitory control and mental flexibility (Jones et al., 2016[21]). Working memory is the ability to store and manipulate or use information in order to complete a task. Inhibitory control (inhibition) represents the ability to overcome strong tendencies to react in a habitual manner, while mental flexibility reflects the capacity to shift between rules or adapt to changing circumstances.

The development of early self-regulation skills enables children to persist in achieving goals and to regulate their behaviour. The latter manifests itself through inhibiting impulsive behaviours and delaying gratification (Mischel, Shoda and Rodriguez, 1989[22]). As well as being better able to achieve tasks, children with self-regulation skills are more able to operate effectively in groups than those with poor behavioural regulation.

Emergent numeracy

Early numeracy skills reflect children's ability to reason and apply simple numerical concepts. Early numeracy comprises the ability to identify and understand numbers, to count, and to detect patterns and shapes. The early numeracy skills that are predictive of later positive outcomes for children are as much about the processes of mathematics as about content. Children at this stage are learning that things can be measured, such as through counting objects and through comparing lengths and weights. At the age of five, children are also developing organised ways of thinking about and dealing with mathematical issues to find solutions.

Social-emotional skills

During their early years, children begin to form close relationships and develop expectations about the behaviour of both themselves and others. They learn to control their emotions and actions, to take others' perspectives and to empathise. These skills represent the basic building blocks for the later development of more complex social-emotional skills. Of particular importance in the early years are children's empathy, trust in people familiar to them and prosocial behaviour, including the absence of disruptive behaviours.

THE DRIVERS OF POSITIVE EARLY DEVELOPMENT

Human development is highly complex and cannot be distilled into simple dichotomies such as the classical "nature versus nurture" debate as individuals and contexts mutually influence one another (Overton, 2015[23]). In other words, children's individual characteristics (i.e. biological or inherited features) constantly interact with the characteristics of their surroundings (e.g. their home and other learning environments). Thus, while skills may be heritable to varying extents, the environments that children experience influence the ways in which they develop particular skills and also their potential for learning new skills (Kovas et al., 2007[24]).

Recent research in neuroscience and brain development (Stiles and Jernigan, 2010[1]) shows that the brain develops rapidly during children's early years. As they grow, these learning capacities slow down and the amount of effort it takes to learn new skills increases. High brain malleability early in life means that young children are especially sensitive to external stimuli, such as the types of interactions they have with their parents and other caregivers. Brain development is sequential and cumulative, so frequent and ongoing positive interactions lead to a virtuous cycle of skills acquisition.

The extraordinary plasticity of children's brains, however, cannot ensure that a sufficient rate of early development and learning actually occurs. Children's learning and continuing development depends on a nurturing and stimulating environment, particularly that provided by their families, which can be supported by early childhood education and care services, other early interventions, and early schooling, as set out in Figure 1.5.

Figure 1.5 **Drivers of children's early learning**

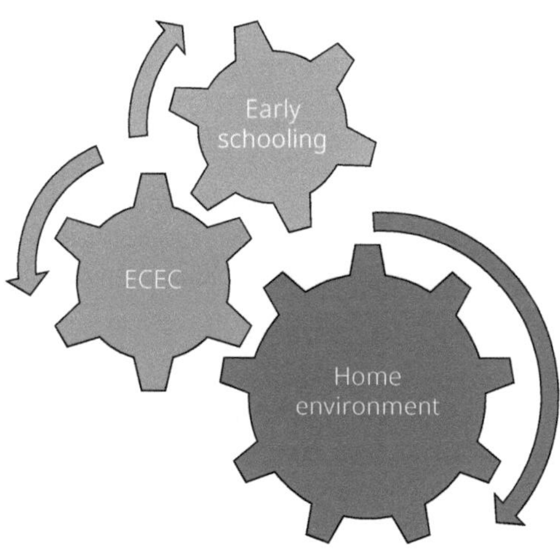

Strong home environments provide a great start for every child

Children's home environments are the strongest predictor of their early development. Their families' socio-economic status, their parents' education, parenting behaviours and parental well-being all contribute to the home environment children experience and thus to their early learning outcomes (Shuey and Kankaraš, 2018[5]).

Parents are children's first teachers. The activities they undertake with their children such as reading to them and engaging them in warm and responsive interactions, and the frequent use of complex adult language creates a home learning environment which supports children's development of cognitive skills, self-regulation, social-emotional skills, and their sense of well-being.

The Effective Pre-school and Primary Education Project (EPPE) found seven parental activities that parents undertake with their children that are significantly associated with later achievement in education. These are:

- frequency of reading from books
- going to the library
- playing with numbers
- painting and drawing
- teaching letters
- teaching numbers, and
- teaching songs, rhymes and poems.

EPPE found the combined effect of these activities on children's development was greater than the effects of parental education or family socio-economic status, although the prevalence of these activities correlated positively with both. Positive home learning environments were associated with stronger cognitive development, self-regulation and social-emotional skills. Thus, what parents do is more important than who they are (Sylva et al., 2004[8]).

Early childhood education and care can enhance early skill development, but it is not guaranteed

ECEC often serves multiple functions. In many countries, it is used as a tool to increase women's labour market participation, help families to reconcile work and family responsibilities, confront demographic challenges such as decreasing fertility rates and aging populations, and maintain high employment rates among the population.

More recently, however, governments have increasingly seen ECEC as a means to support children's early development and mitigate the effects of inequity. Policy makers are increasingly investing in early childhood programmes to build a strong foundation for cognitive and social-emotional skills, especially for children from disadvantaged or immigrant backgrounds to combat the linguistic and economic disadvantages that could otherwise hinder their development and integration. As such, ECEC is seen by many as a critical policy measure that can promote equity, support holistic and continuous development and improve children's well-being.

Results from the Programme for International Student Assessment (PISA) 2018, however, show highly variable effects from students' ECEC participation across countries. Even after taking into account differences in socio-economic background, the effects of participating in early childhood education on students' academic achievement at age 15 differ substantially across countries (Figure 1.6). Some education systems show very positive benefits among students who have attended ECEC whereas in others the impact appears to be neutral or even negative.

While more information is needed to understand these results, it is clear that ECEC does not guarantee better outcomes for students. In addition, the overall benefits of ECEC can diminish in systems where provision has expanded (Duncan and Magnuson, 2013). Thus, increasing provision without information about its quality or impact may not result in better outcomes for children. In fact, there is even evidence that some low-quality ECEC settings may damage children's outcomes and their subsequent prospects (Shuey and Kankaraš, 2018[5]).

Despite growing interest from policy makers on how to use ECEC for the benefit of children, there is little system-level information to help policy makers or education leaders to do so with any level of confidence. The relationship between children's development and structural aspects of ECEC provision, such as group size, has been found to be weak. Even factors such as teachers' qualifications do not always show a clear relationship with children's outcomes (Shuey and Kankaraš, 2018[5]). While process quality[2] is undoubtedly key, there is little evidence about what forms of participation, provision and pedagogical approaches work best for different groups of children.

In addition, in some countries, children from disadvantaged backgrounds have more limited access to ECEC than other children and they access lower-quality provision that is less responsive or tailored to their needs.

Figure 1.6 **Relationship between age of participation in early childhood education programmes and students' reading scores at age 15 across countries, controlling for socio-economic status, 2018**

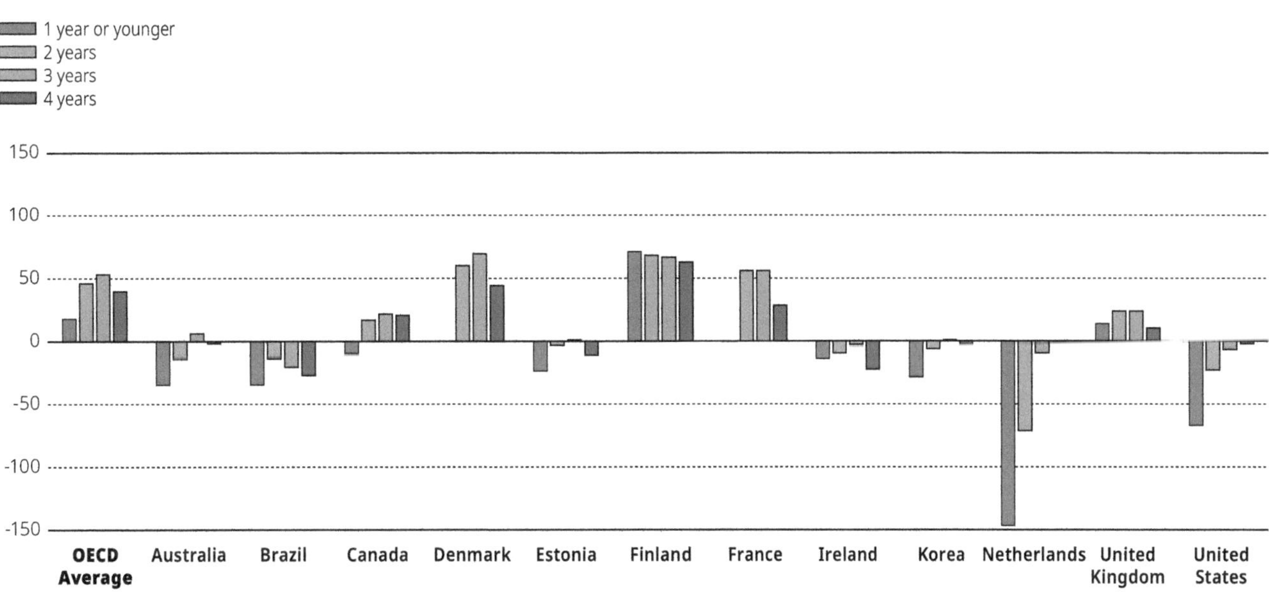

Note: Impact of participation represents score-point difference in reading performance between students who reported having attended pre-school and those who did not. Differences in reading scores take into account students' socio-economic profiles.
Source: OECD (2018[26]) PISA 2018 Database, http://www.oecd.org/pisa/data/2018database/.
StatLink ᵐˢᵖ https://doi.org/10.1787/888934110239

CATCHING-UP DURING EARLY SCHOOLING IS POSSIBLE BUT IS CHALLENGING

High-quality early schooling can partly compensate for children's limited learning and development prior to school. While learning in the early years is more predictive of later outcomes than the first year or two in school, the initial years of schooling can still alter children's later learning trajectories.

Early schooling can be particularly effective in ameliorating poor mathematical skills on school entry. High-quality teaching in the first year or two of school can result in children making rapid progress. However, most children who have weak early numeracy skills do not entirely catch up with their peers who started school with strong early skills in numeracy (Sylva et al., 2008[27]).

High-quality early schooling can also accelerate children's literacy skills and their self-regulation, although not with the same success as in mathematics, and again, these children do not entirely catch up with their peers who started with strong early skills in literacy.

For children from disadvantaged backgrounds, high-quality early schooling is essential if they are to progress well in school - even if they have had a strong early start. Among advantaged children, having strong early skills when they start school provides a protective buffer against mediocre quality early schooling. This is not the case, however, for disadvantaged children. Disadvantaged children with strong early skills at school entry typically fall behind if they experience low-quality teaching in the first year or two of school. Positive outcomes in the earliest years do not entirely eliminate the vulnerability of disadvantage.

Paying attention to the early years reaps benefits for governments

Skills are more important than ever before, not only for individuals, but also for achieving cohesive families, communities and societies. As the value of skills increases across countries, the outlook for people with poor skills becomes a greater concern. Without the means for all citizens to develop the skills they need to fully participate in society, inequity and the by-products of inequity grow.

Inequality has increased across many countries over past decades and the economic recovery since the last financial crisis has exacerbated this. Top and middle-income groups have recovered much of the lost ground whereas those in the bottom income levels are still well below pre-crisis levels (OECD, 2016[28]).

The populations of OECD countries are becoming increasingly heterogeneous as a result of migration. For example, the share of the foreign-born population in OECD countries increased from 6% to 9% over the last two decades. Integrating young immigrant children into their new communities is of key importance for social and economic cohesion (OECD, 2017[29]).

The evidence is overwhelming. ***Starting behind means staying behind.*** When children's early learning is not strong before they start school and continues to be weak in the first two years of school, the outlook for these children is bleak. This group of children is likely to continue to attend school, at least until the end of primary school, but many will not develop the basic academic skills they need to achieve positive labour market outcomes. Some will struggle to participate fully in society or experience positive levels of well-being. This is a particular concern in countries or regions where rates of inequality and deprivation are already high and growing.

Governments can do much to promote early learning and child well-being in early childhood. Policies that support families with young children range from the provision of parental leave, to ensuring access to adequate housing in safe environments, to rules on migration and family reunification. The most direct policy levers available to governments for strengthening early learning are in the realm of ECEC as well as parenting programmes and other supports for families with young children.

Despite the potential for enhancing outcomes through early years policies, some governments know very little about the impact of their early years policies. Reliable, valid, comparable data on children's early learning outcomes and well-being are the only means to gauge how well children are faring and what is most needed to improve children's early experiences and outcomes.

Box 1.1 **Children's rights to early learning and well-being**

The United Nations Declaration on the Rights of the Child (UN, 1959[30]) states that every child should be enabled to develop and learn, to enjoy their early years and be positioned for later success and well-being across all dimensions of their lives. Principle 2 sets out that:

"The child shall … be given opportunities and facilities to enable him (her) to develop physically, mentally, morally, spiritually and socially in a healthy and normal manner … the best interests of the child shall be the paramount consideration."

Principle 6 of the Declaration refers to the importance of children having opportunities for love, understanding, care and security, while Principle 7 refers to opportunities for play and recreation, and an entitlement to education. The Declaration states that education will:

"… promote his (her) general culture and enable him (her), on a basis of equal opportunity, to develop his (her) abilities, his (her) individual judgement, and his (her) sense of moral and social responsibility, and to become a useful member of society."

With similar intent, the Sustainable Development Goals (SDGs) prioritise children's early development. Target 4.2 aspires "to ensure by 2030 that all girls and boys have access to quality early childhood development, care and pre-primary education so that they are ready for primary education".

CONCLUSIONS

Children's well-being during childhood and as they grow into adulthood is significantly influenced by their experiences in the first few years of their lives. The development of children's early cognitive and social-emotional skills has long-lasting impacts on their later physical and mental health, life satisfaction, educational attainment, employment, income, and civic engagement. The benefits of strong early learning among children are clearly evident when they start school, at the end of compulsory education and later in adulthood. When children do not develop critical early skills, however, their well-being during childhood is undermined and they face enormous challenges in achieving positive outcomes as adults.

Countries will make faster progress on improving children's early learning experiences if they are able to learn from other countries and systems, rather than each working in isolation. There is a lack of reliable, valid and comparable international evidence that enables countries to do so. The International Early Learning and Child Well-being Study (IELS) addresses this gap.

References

Bartik, T. (2014), *From Preschool to Prosperity: The Economic Payoff to Early Childhood Education*, W.E. Upjohn Institute, http://dx.doi.org/10.17848/9780880994835. [6]

Cunha, F. and **J. Heckman** (2009), *The Economics and Psychology of Inequality and Human Development*, National Bureau of Economic Research, Cambridge, MA, http://dx.doi.org/10.3386/w14695. [7]

Duncan, G. et al. (2007), "School Readiness and Later Achievement", *Psychological Association*, Vol. 43/6, pp. 1428-1446, http://dx.doi.org/10.1037/[0012-1649.43.6.1428].supp. [10]

Fergusson, D., J. Boden and **L. Horwood** (2013), "Childhood self-control and adult outcomes: Results from a 30-year longitudinal study", *Journal of the American Academy of Child and Adolescent Psychiatry*, Vol. 52/7, pp. 709-717.e1, http://dx.doi.org/10.1016/j.jaac.2013.04.008. [19]

Fontaine, N. et al. (2011), "Predictors and outcomes of joint trajectories of callous–unemotional traits and conduct problems in childhood.", *Journal of Abnormal Psychology*, Vol. 120/3, pp. 730-742, http://dx.doi.org/10.1037/a0022620. [20]

Heckman, J. (2006), *Skill formation and the economics of investing in disadvantaged children*, http://dx.doi.org/10.1126/science.1128898. [3]

Heckman, J. and **G. Karapukula** (2019), *Intergenerational and Intragenerational Externalities of the Perry Preschool Project*, https://papers.ssrn.com/sol3/papers.cfm?abstract_id=3399272 (accessed on 25 February 2020). [16]

Jones, S. et al. (2016), *EXECUTIVE FUNCTION MAPPING PROJECT: Untangling the Terms and Skills Related to Executive Function and Self-Regulation in Early Childhood*, http://www.acf.hhs.gov/programs/opre/index.html. (accessed on 25 February 2020). [21]

Kovas, Y. et al. (2007), "The genetic and environmental origins of learning abilites and disabilities in the early school years", *Monographs of the Society for Research in Child Development*, Vol. 72/3, pp. 1-144, http://dx.doi.org/10.1111/j.1540-5834.2007.00439.x. [24]

Li-Grining, C. et al. (2010), "Children's Early Approaches to Learning and Academic Trajectories Through Fifth Grade", *Developmental Psychology*, Vol. 46/5, pp. 1062-1077, http://dx.doi.org/10.1037/a0020066. [11]

McClelland, M. et al. (2013), "Relations between preschool attention span-persistence and age 25 educational outcomes", *Early Childhood Research Quarterly*, Vol. 28/2, pp. 314-324, http://dx.doi.org/10.1016/j.ecresq.2012.07.008. [14]

Melhuish, E. et al. (2008), "Effects of the Home Learning Environment and Preschool Center Experience upon Literacy and Numeracy Development in Early Primary School", *Journal of Social Issues*, Vol. 64/1, pp. 95-114, http://dx.doi.org/10.1111/j.1540-4560.2008.00550.x. [25]

Mischel, W., Y. Shoda and **M. Rodriguez** (1989), "Delay of gratification in children", *Science*, Vol. 244/4907, pp. 933-938, http://dx.doi.org/10.1126/science.2658056. [22]

Moffitt, T. et al. (2011), "A gradient of childhood self-control predicts health, wealth, and public safety", *Proceedings of the National Academy of Sciences of the United States of America*, Vol. 108/7, pp. 2693-2698, http://dx.doi.org/10.1073/pnas.1010076108. [18]

Neuenschwander, R. et al. (2012), "How do different aspects of self-regulation predict successful adaptation to school?", *Journal of Experimental Child Psychology*, Vol. 113/3, pp. 353-371, http://dx.doi.org/10.1016/j.jecp.2012.07.004. [12]

OECD (2019), *Education at a Glance 2019: OECD Indicators*, OECD Publishing, Paris, https://dx.doi.org/10.1787/f8d7880d-en. [4]

OECD (2018), *PISA 2018 Database*, http://www.oecd.org/pisa/data/2018database/ (accessed on 26 January 2020). [26]

OECD (2017), *Starting Strong 2017 Key Indicators on Early Childhood Education and Care*, https://dx.doi.org/10.1787/9789264276116-en (accessed on 25 February 2020). [29]

OECD (2020), *Income inequality update* (indicator), https://dx.doi.org/10.1787/459aa7f1-en (accessed on 25 February 2020). [28]

Overton, W. (2015), "Processes, Relations, and Relational-Developmental-Systems", in *Handbook of Child Psychology and Developmental Science*, John Wiley & Sons, Inc., http://dx.doi.org/10.1002/9781118963418.childpsy102. [23]

Parsons, S. et al. (2011), "Long-term outcomes for children with early language problems: Beating the odds", *Children and Society*, Vol. 25/3, pp. 202-214, http://dx.doi.org/10.1111/j.1099-0860.2009.00274.x. [17]

Schoon, I. et al. (2015), *The Impact of Early Life Skills on Later Outcomes*, http://discovery.ucl.ac.uk/10051902/1/Schoon_2015%20The%20Impact%20of%20Early%20Life%20Skills%20on%20Later%20Outcomes_%20Sept%20fin2015.pdf (accessed on 31 July 2019). [15]

Shuey, E. and **M. Kankaraš** (2018), "The Power and Promise of Early Learning", *OECD Education Working Papers*, No. 186, OECD Publishing, Paris, https://dx.doi.org/10.1787/f9b2e53f-en. [5]

Siraj, I. et al. (2017), *Fostering Effective Early Learning Study A review of the current international evidence considering quality in early childhood education and care programmes-in delivery, pedagogy and child outcomes*, NSW Government, http://www.dec.nsw.gov.au (accessed on 25 February 2020). [9]

Stiles, J. and **T. Jernigan** (2010), *The basics of brain development*, http://dx.doi.org/10.1007/s11065-010-9148-4. [1]

Sylva, K. et al. (2008), "Final report from the primary phase: Pre-school, school and family influences on children's development during Key Stage 2 (7-11)", *Faculty of Social Sciences - Papers*, https://ro.uow.edu.au/sspapers/1807 (accessed on 25 February 2020). [27]

Sylva, K. et al. (2004), *The Effective Provision of Pre-School Education (EPPE) Project: Findings from Pre-school to end of Key Stage1*, http://www.ioe.ac.uk/projects/eppe (accessed on 5 December 2019). [8]

UN (1959), Declaration of the Rights of the Child (1959), https://www.ohchr.org/EN/Issues/Education/Training/Compilation/Pages/1DeclarationoftheRightsoftheChild(1959).aspx, (accessed 4 March 2020). [30]

Walker, S. (2011), "Early childhood stimulation benefits adult competence and reduces violent behavior", *Pediatrics*, Vol. 127/5, pp. 849-857, http://dx.doi.org/10.1542/peds.2010-2231. [2]

Washbrook, E., C. Propper and **K. Sayal** (2013), "Pre-school hyperactivity/attention problems and educational outcomes in adolescence: Prospective longitudinal study", *British Journal of Psychiatry*, Vol. 203/4, pp. 265-271, http://dx.doi.org/10.1192/bjp.bp.112.123562. [13]

Notes

1. For a fuller description of relevant longitudinal studies refer to Shuey and Kankaraš (2018[5]).

2. Process quality refers to the quality of pedagogical interactions between ECEC staff and children, the quality of communications between staff and parents, and most importantly, the quality of interactions among children, as well as the quality of interaction of children with space and material (OECD, 2017[29]).

The design and implementation of the study

The International Early Learning and Child Well-Being Study (IELS) was designed in conjunction with both participating and interested countries. This chapter outlines key elements of the design and implementation of the study. This includes the objectives and guiding principles for the study, as well as the target group of children sampled, the aspects of children's early learning that were assessed, how the assessments were carried out, and the contextual information gathered on each child.

The International Early Learning and Child Well-being Study (IELS) has been developed to inform countries' efforts to improve children's early learning and well-being. To achieve this goal, the study was designed in conjunction with participating and interested countries, to ensure the approach responded well to their policy needs. The fundamental objective of the study is to provide countries with reliable, valid and comparable data they can use to benchmark and monitor the performance of their systems in giving all children a strong early start.

This chapter outlines the key features of the overall design and implementation of the study, including:

- objectives and guiding principles
- the conceptual design of the study
- the target group of children sampled in the study
- the aspects of children's early learning that were assessed
- how children were assessed
- contextual information gathered on each child
- how the study was implemented in the participating countries.

OBJECTIVES AND GUIDING PRINCIPLES

The overarching objective of IELS is to support countries in their efforts to improve children's early learning experiences, to better foster their early development and overall well-being (Box 2.1). Children's early learning is a strong determinant of their later success in life, across a range of outcomes. As outlined in Chapter 1, sound early learning correlates with positive benefits in later educational achievement and attainment, employment and earnings, mental and physical health, citizenship, well-being and life satisfaction.

Box 2.1 **Policy and research questions addressed by the study**

IELS was designed to answer the following policy and research questions for each participating country:

- How well are children developing the skills they need, for their well-being and ongoing positive outcomes?
- To what extent are children developing a sound balance of cognitive and social-emotional skills?
- How much variation is there in children's outcomes?
- How are different groups of children faring, such as:
  - boys versus girls?
  - children from different socio-economic backgrounds?
  - children from migrant families?
  - children who speak a home language that is different from that spoken in their ECEC centre or school?
- What factors are positively or negatively associated with children's early learning and development?

The vast majority of children who have poor cognitive and social-emotional skills at the age of seven will not catch up with their peers who had a better start in their early years and will face poorer outcomes in schooling and in later life (Stiles and Jernigan, 2010[1]). For many of these children, these poorer outcomes could have been averted if they had received tailored, high-quality interventions in their early years and in the first year or two of early schooling. As children move through primary school, it is increasingly difficult to significantly ameliorate or eliminate learning gaps through, for example, remedial education or other interventions (Shuey and Kankaraš, 2018[2]).

Education systems with a larger proportion of children with poor early development are limited in the extent to which they can achieve success for these children and can perform well overall, as a system. Ensuring as many children as possible develop well in their early years will provide system-level benefits for society as a whole, as well as improving outcomes for individual children and their families.

IELS enables countries to understand how well different groups of children are developing, including any significant differences between girls and boys, socio-economic groups, and children from migrant or linguistically diverse backgrounds.

IELS helps countries to consider where it might be possible to make improvements to enhance children's early years experiences and outcomes. International comparative data helps policy makers, education leaders and practitioners, and parents to see what can be achieved for children in the early years. This includes key system goals such as mitigating disadvantage and ensuring children are well-positioned to succeed in school. Thus, IELS provides countries with a common language and framework to learn from each other, to improve the relative effectiveness and equity of their approaches and systems.

IELS also provides countries with insights into the focus needed in early primary school. Much can still be done to enhance five-year-olds' cognitive and social-emotional development, but this will depend on the extent to which early schooling is oriented towards children's actual development needs and can effectively meet them.

As noted above, the study was developed in conjunction with countries interested in children's early learning and well-being. As well as setting the objectives for the study, countries agreed on a set of guiding principles to steer the design, development and implementation of the study. These were that the study would be:

- *Ethical* - ensuring the well-being of children in the study was paramount in all decisions, including developmentally appropriate assessments

- *Policy relevant* - responding to the policy questions above and enabling changes in policy and/or practices

- *Feasible* - straightforward to implement

- *Reliable, valid and comparable* - across countries, languages, cultural contexts and over time

- *Efficient* - limiting the burden on practitioners and parents, as well as on children

- *Cost effective* – affordable for a range of countries

- *Sustainable* – establishing strong foundations to enable multiple cycles.

THE CONCEPTUAL DESIGN OF THE STUDY

The study focuses on those aspects of children's early learning that have been found to best predict positive later outcomes. These later outcomes include educational achievement and attainment, mental and physical health, employment and earnings, citizenship, wider well-being and life satisfaction.

The areas of early learning that best support positive later outcomes are inter-related and mutually reinforcing. This core set of early learning encompasses emergent literacy, emergent numeracy, self-regulation, and social-emotional skills.

The study also captures relevant contextual information relating to children's individual characteristics, family and home environments, and their early childhood education and care (ECEC) experiences.

These elements are set out diagrammatically in Figure 2.1.

Figure 2.1 **Conceptual framework for the study**

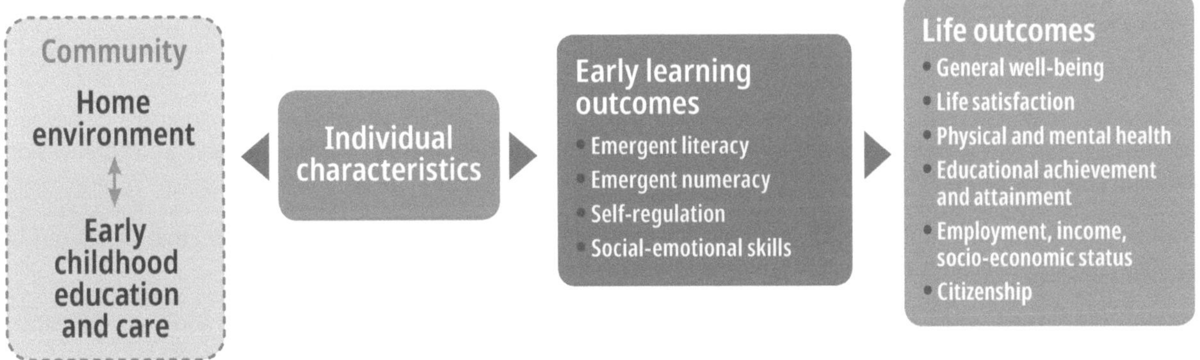

THE TARGET GROUP OF CHILDREN SAMPLED IN THE STUDY

The children included in the study were all five years old and in regulated ECEC settings or in school. The survey took a representative sample of children in each participating country. To achieve nationally representative samples, a two-stage probability design was used. In the first stage, a random sample of ECEC centres or schools was selected in each country. In the second stage, children were randomly selected from the list of children who met the age requirements within each of the selected settings. Overall, just under 7 000 children took part in the study.

The assessments were carried out among children at a common age, rather than at a particular stage of education, in order to provide comparability across countries. A stage of education refers to a level or step within an education system, such as the point of entry into school or the last year of ECEC. Stages of education vary across countries and even within countries in some cases. For example, the age of school entry can vary by as much as three years across education systems. Given that the policy and research questions the study is addressing relate to children's outcomes, from a system perspective, focusing on a common age rather than a common stage gives a better basis for comparison across diverse systems.

Five years is the age at which there is near-universal participation in some form of formal setting in most OECD countries. While some countries have not yet achieved universal participation at this age, most are progressing towards universality as a result of increasing rates of participation in ECEC and younger ages of entry into schooling.

It is simpler and more reliable to carry out the assessment process with five-year-olds than with children who are two years younger or even one year younger. At the age of five, children are able to follow directions and complete straight-forward activities with little assistance.

From a system perspective, five years is often the age when children are about to enter the school system. Comparative assessment information at this point will therefore help countries to later gauge the impact their schooling systems are having on children's later educational outcomes.

The children were assessed in the regulated ECEC centre or school they attended, to ensure the assessment was carried out in a setting the child was familiar with and for reasons of practicality and cost. Accessing children in formal settings is easier and less costly than locating children and undertaking the assessments in the child's home or in another type of setting.

THE ASPECTS OF CHILDREN'S EARLY LEARNING THAT WERE ASSESSED

The early learning domains included in IELS are comprehensive and reflect the critical skills children need for their ongoing learning and well-being. As noted above, children's learning in different domains is inter-related and mutually reinforcing. Children who are developing well in one area, such as self-regulation, are likely to also be developing in other areas such as emergent numeracy and prosocial skills. While all areas of children's development matter, the inter-related and overlapping nature of early learning domains means it is not necessary to measure every skill to have an accurate indication of how well a child is developing. Nonetheless, some early learning domains are more predictive than others in terms of children's later outcomes and some also have greater independent effects on children's later development than other domains.

The three key aspects of children's early learning selected for the study each have significant effects on children's development trajectories and also have independent effects. They were:

- cognitive skills: emergent literacy and emergent numeracy

- self-regulation, and

- social-emotional skills.

In the early years, emergent literacy is predictive of children's later cognitive and social-emotional development (Shuey and Kankaraš, 2018[2]). IELS has therefore focused on key components of emergent literacy, including listening comprehension, vocabulary and phonological awareness.

Key early numeracy skills reflect children's ability to identify and understand numbers, an understanding that things can be counted, measured and compared, and an ability to detect patterns and shapes.

Children's early skills in self-regulation - generally known as executive function - involve remembering and applying information, regulating impulsive behaviours, persisting in tasks and being able to adapt to different rules or circumstances.

Critical early social-emotional skills are those that enable children to form close relationships with others, manage their emotions and actions, and take others' perspectives. Of particular importance in the early years are children's levels of emergent empathy, trust and prosocial behaviour.

The aspects of children's early learning that are included in the study are set out in Figure 2.2.

Figure 2.2 Children's early learning included in IELS

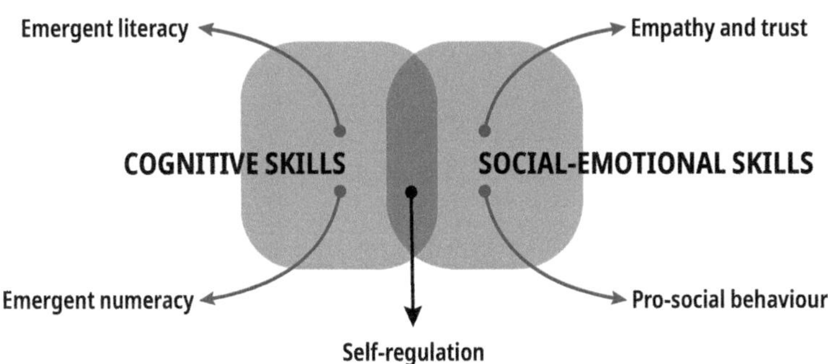

Children who are progressing well across the above areas will be well positioned to form positive relationships with others, succeed in school and experience positive well-being.

HOW CHILDREN WERE ASSESSED

Three sources of information provided a triangulated perspective on each child's learning and development:

- a direct assessment of each child's skills

- feedback from each child's parents on the child's learning, development and behaviour

- feedback from each child's teacher on the child's learning, development and behaviour.

An explanation of each of these three sources of assessment information is provided below.

Direct assessment of each child's skills

Children completed the direct assessment on tablets, with one-to-one support from a trained study administrator. The children listened to stories and engaged with cartoon-like characters in these stories by touching or moving items on the screen. The children were able to go at their own pace, for example when moving to a new screen or to a new activity.

The process was simple and intuitive, and was trialled with different groups of children before the study was implemented in the participating countries. Children did not need any prior experience with tablets or other digital devices to successfully complete the assessment.

The study administrators ensured each activity was ready before children started and that the children could navigate their way through the activities. The study administrator remained with the child throughout the assessment.

Each assessment activity took approximately 15 minutes. Two assessment activities were administered per day, across two days. The two-day format worked well for children and there was little attrition of children across the two days.

The stories and other activities the children engaged in during the assessment were interesting, fun and developmentally appropriate for this age group. Two characters – Tom and Mia – guided the children via audio through the activities (Figure 2.3). The names and physical characteristics of these lead characters were adapted to the context of each participating country. There was no reading or writing involved in the direct assessment activities, only visual and audio materials.

As well as being easy to navigate and engaging for children, the digital design of the direct assessment made the results more accurate than they would have been with paper based or observational models of assessment. It also meant the assessment process was more efficient to administer.

Information from parents and teachers

The children's parents and the teacher or ECEC staff member who knew them best were asked to provide information on their learning and development. This enabled the study to triangulate the information gathered from the direct assessments and indirect assessments, and also gauge children's development across a broader scope of domains than is possible solely through a direct assessment.

Figure 2.3 **Tom and Mia, the lead characters from the children's stories in IELS**

Parents and teachers provided information on the same skills covered by the direct assessment as well as on a broader set of skills and behaviours. They answered questions on the children's capacity to complete a series of cognitive tasks (assessing their emergent literacy and emergent numeracy), the social-emotional skills and behaviour that they observed at home or at the ECEC centre or school the children attended.

For example, they were asked how often each child:

- joins in with other children playing (prosocial behaviour)

- approaches familiar adults for comfort when upset (trust)

- fights with other children (disruptive behaviour).

Parents and teachers could answer "never", "rarely", "sometimes", "often" or "always".

CONTEXTUAL INFORMATION ON EACH CHILD

Contextual information on children's home environments and ECEC history is critical for understanding how children's skills develop and how they can be better supported. This information was collected in addition to information on the individual characteristics of each child. The study gathered contextual information about three key areas.

The individual characteristics of each child

The study collected information about the individual characteristics of the children participating in the study, including their exact ages, gender, any special learning or behavioural needs, and whether they had a low birthweight or had been premature.

Home environment

Children's home environments also affect their development and well-being. For this reason, the study collected information from parents on:

- the socio-economic status of the family, i.e. parental occupation, parents' level of education, household income

- household composition, e.g. whether it was a one or two parent household and number of siblings

- the immigration background of the family[1]

- the language/s spoken in the home

- the activities parents undertake with the children such as reading to them from books and having back-and-forth conversations

- access to and frequency of use of digital devices.

Early childhood education and care experiences

The children's parents were also asked whether their child had previously participated in ECEC. If so, they were then asked for further details about the types of ECEC their child had participated in, the age the child started ECEC, and whether the child attended more or fewer than 20 hours a week, for each year the child attended ECEC.

HOW THE STUDY WAS IMPLEMENTED

Three OECD countries participated in this study: England (United Kingdom), Estonia and the United States. The study was implemented in each country by a national study centre set up for this purpose. Each country appointed a national project manager to oversee all aspects of implementation. These included:

- recruiting centres/schools and children to meet sample requirements

- translations, e.g. into Estonian and Russian

- adaptations, to reflect the context of the country or adding additional questions of particular interest to an individual country

- recruiting and training study administrators

- providing resources for the study, e.g. tablets.

Each child in the study was supported on a one-to-one basis throughout the direct assessment by a trained study administrator. The primary role of the study administrators was to ensure the well-being of each child throughout the assessment. They showed children how to navigate the tablet and took them through practice exercises at the beginning of the process to ensure they were ready to start the assessment.

Study administrators remained with the children until they had completed the assessment activities. They ensured the children were happy to continue at each stage of the assessment process and that they took a break between assessment activities, if they wanted to. Study administrators did not guide children on how to respond to the activities, but did help any child who was unsure what to do next, such as how to move to the next screen.

The implementation of the study was monitored in each participating country by international quality monitors. These experts attested that implementation complied with the international quality standards for the study. All three participating countries met these standards.

PARTICIPATION RATES

Participation rates in the study among children, teachers and parents were exceptionally high, compared to similar studies[2]. Parents readily provided their consent for their children to participate and also completed the survey questionnaire in high numbers.

Response rates from teachers were also high, at 90% or higher in each country, and there appeared to be no concerns amongst teachers about their participation or the time required to complete the questionnaire. In visits the OECD Secretariat made to each participating country at the end of 2018, a number of heads and teachers from participating schools and centres told them that they believed more attention needs to be given to this age group and that an international study of this nature would achieve this goal. They also noted their support for the balanced focus of the study across children's cognitive and social-emotional skills.

References

Shuey, E. and **M. Kankaraš** (2018), "The Power and Promise of Early Learning", *OECD Education Working Papers*, No. 186, OECD Publishing, Paris, https://dx.doi.org/10.1787/f9b2e53f-en.   [2]

Stiles, J. and **T. Jernigan** (2010), *The basics of brain development*, http://dx.doi.org/10.1007/s11065-010-9148-4.   [1]

Notes

1. Defined has having two parents who were born in a country or economy other than that in which the child participated in IELS (or one parent, in the case where information on only one parent was provided).

2. Further information on participation rates can be found in the Technical Annex to this report.

A snapshot of participating countries

This chapter provides contextual information on the three participating countries: England (United Kingdom), Estonia and the United States. This information includes demographic characteristics and trends, income and inequalities, and systems to support children's early learning and well-being. In addition, the chapter provides information on the relative performance of each country's education system.

3

INTRODUCTION

The International Early Learning and Child Well-being Study (IELS) was implemented in three OECD countries: England (United Kingdom), Estonia and the United States, and the findings from this study are based on just under 7 000 five-year-olds in these three countries.

The participating countries in this study have a number of similarities, but there are also important differences between them. England, Estonia and the United States all have well-established education systems. Nonetheless, they differ in terms of scale, wealth, demographics, diversity and education performance at a system-level. There are also significant differences in each country's early learning systems and the other support they provide to children and their families.

Recognising these differences helps to better understand the findings across countries, such as the extent to which each is able to mitigate disadvantage as well as the overall results for each country. The characteristics of each country provide the background and context for the study's country-specific findings, as these affect the context in which the five-year-old children in this study are growing up, such as the families and communities in which they live.

This chapter outlines key differences between England[1], Estonia and the United States from a system perspective. The factors considered include demographics, income levels, early years systems, education levels and education system performance.

DEMOGRAPHICS

The three countries are very different in scale

The United States has the largest population of any OECD country, estimated at just under 320 million people in 2014. This is more than five times the population of England, estimated at 56 million in 2018,[2] and far greater than Estonia, which had an estimated population of just over 1 million in 2019. Estonia is one of the smallest countries in the OECD, as Figure 3.1 shows.

Figure 3.1 **Total population across OECD countries**

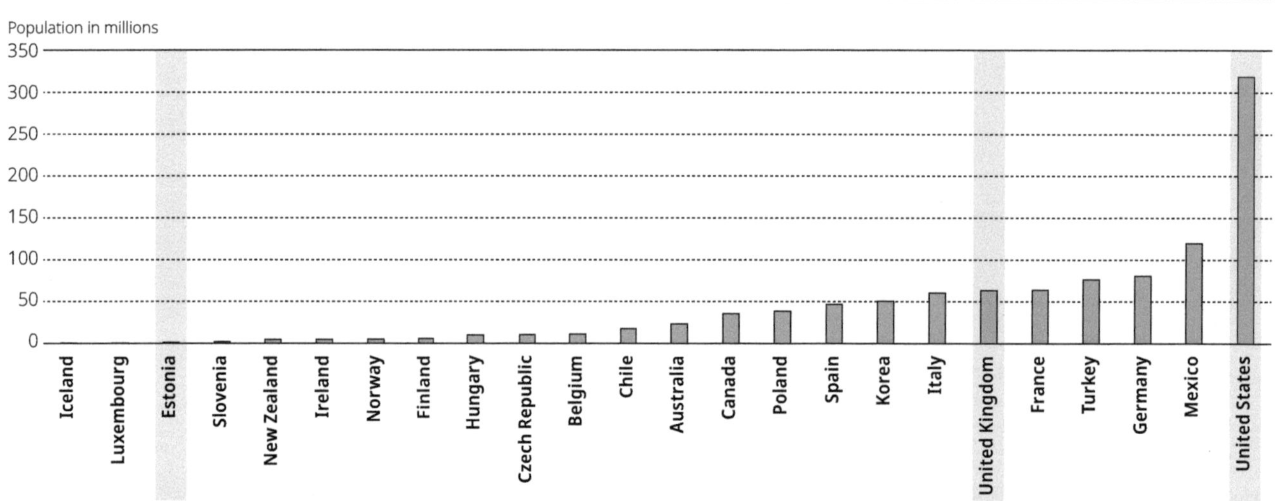

Source: (OECD, 2020[1]), Population (indicator), https://doi.org/10.1787/d434f82b-en

StatLink https://doi.org/10.1787/888934110258

In 2017, there were 24 million children aged five and under in the United States, compared to 3 million children in that age group in England and 54 000 children in Estonia.

In 2017, fertility rates across the three countries were 1.59 for Estonia, 1.76 for England and 1.77 for the United States, compared to the OECD average of 1.70. These relative rates are reflected in the proportion of the population who are under the age of 15: 15.8% in Estonia, 17.8% in the United Kingdom and 19.2% in the United States. (OECD, 2020[1]).

In addition to fertility rates, factors such as migration and mortality rates also influence overall population levels and the size of the working-age population. In 2018, both the United Kingdom and the United States experienced population growth of 0.7%, whereas Estonia experienced negative growth of -0.2%. The proportion of the working-age population – defined as those aged 15 to 64 years – appears to be declining in Estonia (at 65.8% in 2014) and in the United Kingdom (64.9% in 2014), whereas it has been relatively stable in the United States (at 66.4%) (OECD, 2020[1]).

Skills levels are important for achieving positive economic and social outcomes in any country. However, skill levels become even more critical in economies where the working-age population is in decline and cannot be easily offset through increased inflows of highly skilled migrants.

The United States and England have more diverse populations than Estonia

The United States is more ethnically diverse than England and much more so than Estonia. In 2017, 51% of children in the United States were White, 25% were Hispanic, 14% were Black, 5% were Asian, and 0.8% were American Indian or Alaska Native (Federal Interagency Forum on Child and Family Statistics, 2018[2]). England's population is also diverse, although 75% of children are White, with significant populations of Asian (10%), Black (5%) and mixed race (5%) (Office for National Statistics, 2011). In contrast, Estonia is relatively homogenous, with the only key differences being between Estonian-speaking (70%) and Russian-speaking children (25%) (Statistics Estonia, 2019[3]).

Both the United States and England have significant migrant populations. Among the children included in this study, 18% of children in the United States and in England were from a migrant background, compared to 2% in Estonia.

The language that children and their families speak is a highly relevant factor in relation to diversity and education. Of those sampled for the study, 20% of children in the United States were recorded as having a home language other than English, compared to 16% in England; 6% of the children sampled in Estonia spoke a language other than Estonian or Russian.

Families are becoming increasingly diverse, especially in the United States and England

While most children in OECD countries (82%) still live in two-parent families, family composition has been changing. For example, informal cohabitation has increased from 10% to 16% in the last 10 years. Children are now more likely to experience different family settings during their childhood than previous generations, including living with step-parents and social parents (informal cohabitation);[3] commuting between the homes of their two biological parents; and having half siblings, step-siblings and social siblings (OECD, 2019).

Family composition differs across countries, including the three countries in this study. The United States has a larger proportion of children living in single-parent households than England or Estonia, yet also has a larger proportion of children living with married parents (Figure 3.2).

Figure 3.2 **Distribution of 0-17 year-olds by family structure across OECD countries**

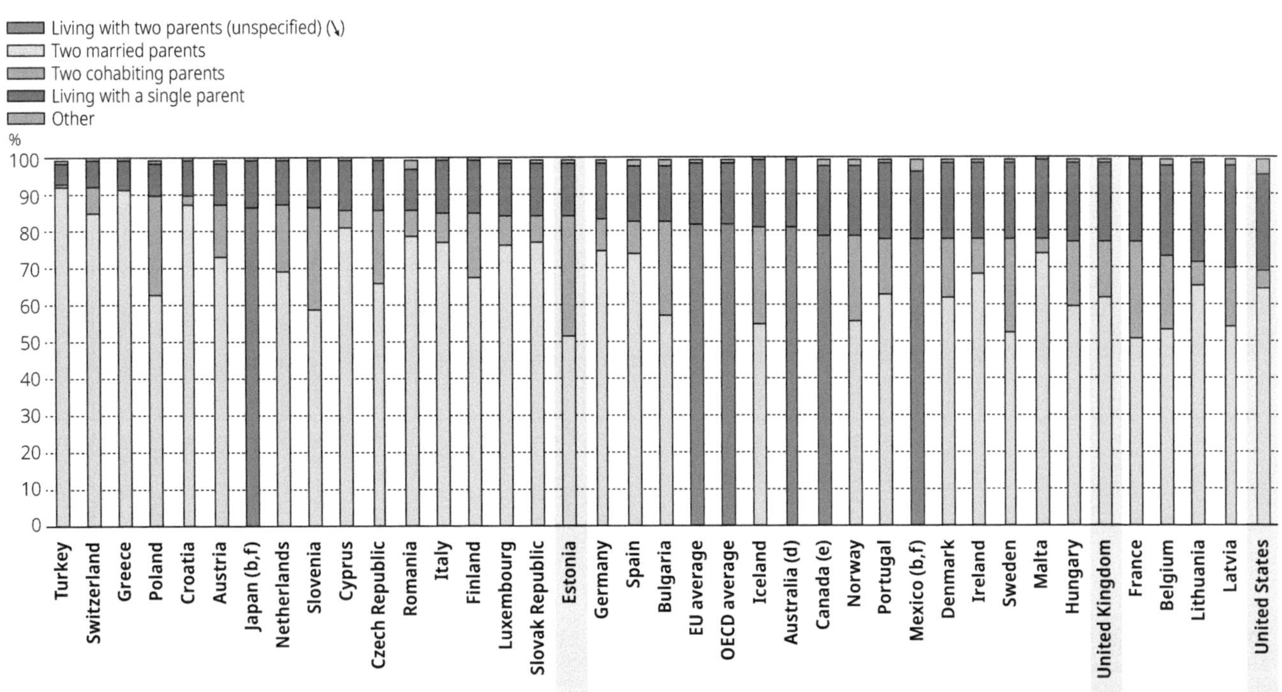

Notes: a) For Japan and Mexico, children aged 0-14; b) 'Parents' generally refers to both biological parents and step-, adoptive parents. 'Living with two married parents' refers to situations where a child lives in a household with two adults that are considered parents and these parents are married to each other or have a registered partnership. 'Living with two cohabiting parents' refers to situations where a child lives in a household with two adults who are considered parents and who are cohabiting without being married nor registered. 'Living with a single parent' refers to situations where a child lives in a household with only one adult who is considered a parent. 'Other' refers to a situation where the child lives without any parent; c) Data for Mexico refer to 2010, for Australia to 2012, for Japan to 2015, for Canada and Iceland to 2016, and for France, Hungary, Ireland, Luxembourg, Turkey, Slovak Republic, and Switzerland refer to 2017.
Source: (OECD, 2019[4]) *Treating all children equally? Why policies should adapt to evolving family realities*, Policy Brief on Child Well-being, OECD. https://www.oecd.org/els/family/child-well-being/Treating-all-children-equally-Policy-brief-2019.pdf, Figure 1.
StatLink ⧉ https://doi.org/10.1787/888934110277

Children have greater access to digital technology

Another change in children's lives is access to digital technology. In 2018, 20% of 15-year-olds who took the Programme for International Student Assessment (PISA) reported that they had had access to the Internet before the age of six years, up 5 percentage points from 2012. As Table 3.1 shows, on average, 83% of children sampled for this study across the three participating countries used a digital device at least once a week, with 42% using such a device every day. Only 7% of children on average never or hardly ever used a device, with 10% of children using a device at least monthly, but not weekly. The use of digital devices was more prevalent in the United States and least prevalent in Estonia.

Table 3.1 **Use of digital devices among five-year-olds by country**

	Every day	At least weekly but not daily	At least monthly but not weekly	Rarely or never
England	39%	46%	9%	6%
Estonia	39%	39%	13%	9%
United States	49%	40%	7%	5%
Overall mean	42%	41%	10%	7%

INCOME

The United States has significantly higher income than the other two countries

The United States has one of the highest gross domestic product (GDP)[4] per capita in the OECD (Figure 3.3). Per capita GDP in the United Kingdom is close to the OECD average, while Estonia's is below the OECD average. The resources of the United States and, to a lesser extent, the United Kingdom therefore exceed Estonia's, influencing the resources available, on average, to individual households and the potential resources available for early years education.

Figure 3.3 **GDP per capita across OECD countries**

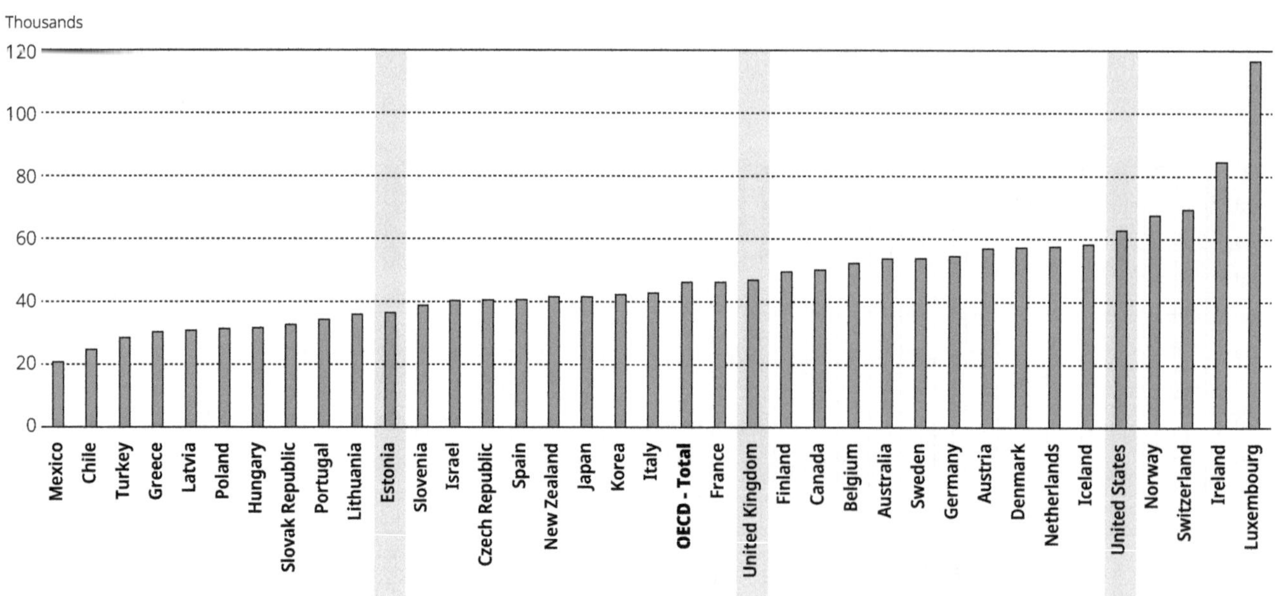

Source: (OECD, 2019[5]) OECD.Stat *Level of GDP per capita and productivity*, https://stats.oecd.org/Index.aspx?DataSetCode=PDB_LV
StatLink https://doi.org/10.1787/888934110296

Estonia has greater income equality

While Estonia has lower per capita GDP than England or the United States, it does not experience the same disparity in wealth or poverty as England or the United States. Figure 3.4 shows the Gini coefficient across OECD countries, where 0 equates to perfect income equality and 1 to perfect inequality.

Figure 3.4 **Gini coefficient across OECD countries**

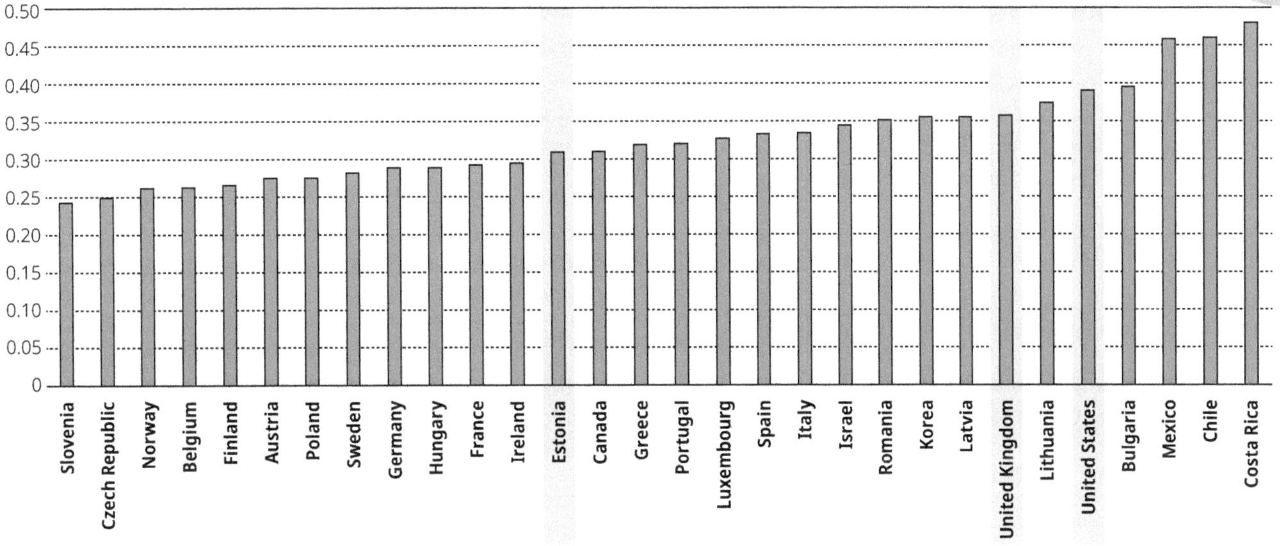

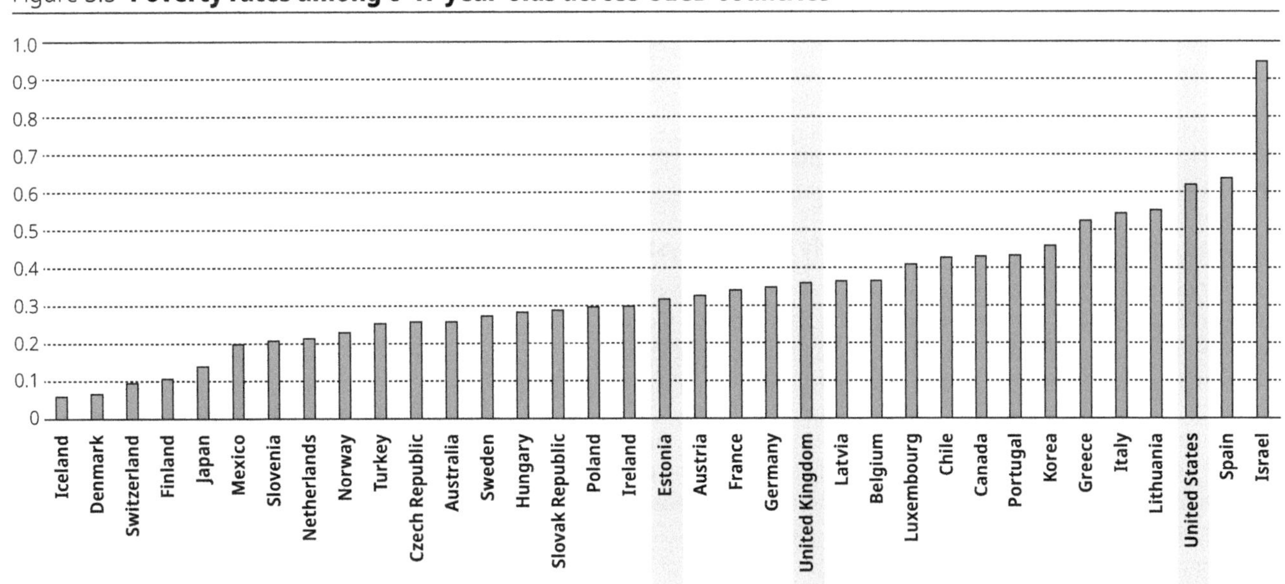

Source: (OECD, 2019[6]), Income inequality (indicator). https://doi.org/10.1787/459aa7f1-en

StatLink https://doi.org/10.1787/888934110315

Estonia also has lower rates of child poverty

Child poverty[5] rates in Estonia are less than half the rates in the United States and a little lower than in the United Kingdom (OECD, 2019[7]). One-fifth of children aged under 18 live in poverty in the United States (21%), compared to 12% in the United Kingdom and 10% in Estonia (Figure 3.5). In the United States, 36% of American Indian/Alaska Native children, 34% of Black children, and 26% of Hispanic children live in poverty, a much larger share than among White children (12%). In England, Black children and children from ethnic minority families are almost twice as likely to live in poverty as children from White families (Department of Work and Pensions, UK Government, 2019[8]).

Figure 3.5 **Poverty rates among 0-17 year-olds across OECD countries**

Source: (OECD, 2019[7]) Poverty rate (indicator). https://doi.org/10.1787/0fe1315d-en

StatLink https://doi.org/10.1787/888934110334

3

EARLY YEARS SYSTEMS

Parents enjoy greater support in England and Estonia than in the United States

England provides paid parental leave of 39 weeks, more than the OECD average of 18 weeks, while Estonia provides 87 weeks of paid parental leave. Total parental leave entitlement in England is 52 weeks compared with 3 years in Estonia. In contrast, the United States is unique among OECD countries in having no statutory entitlement to paid maternity, paternity or parental leave. Large employers in the United States are required to provide 12 weeks unpaid leave and some states and some employers opt to provide longer paid and/or unpaid parental leave for employees.

Parental support helps new parents to care for their children and provide them with a positive early start. The World Health Organization recommends infants should be breastfed for the first 6 months for optimal health, growth and development, including for early cognitive development. In Estonia, 72% of babies are still breastfed at 6 months, compared to 58% in the United States and 36% in England (UNICEF, 2019[9]).

Infant mortality rates are another indicator of how well families and infants are faring. Infant mortality rates are significantly lower in Estonia than in the United Kingdom or the United States (Figure 3.6).

Figure 3.6 **Infant mortality rates across OECD countries**

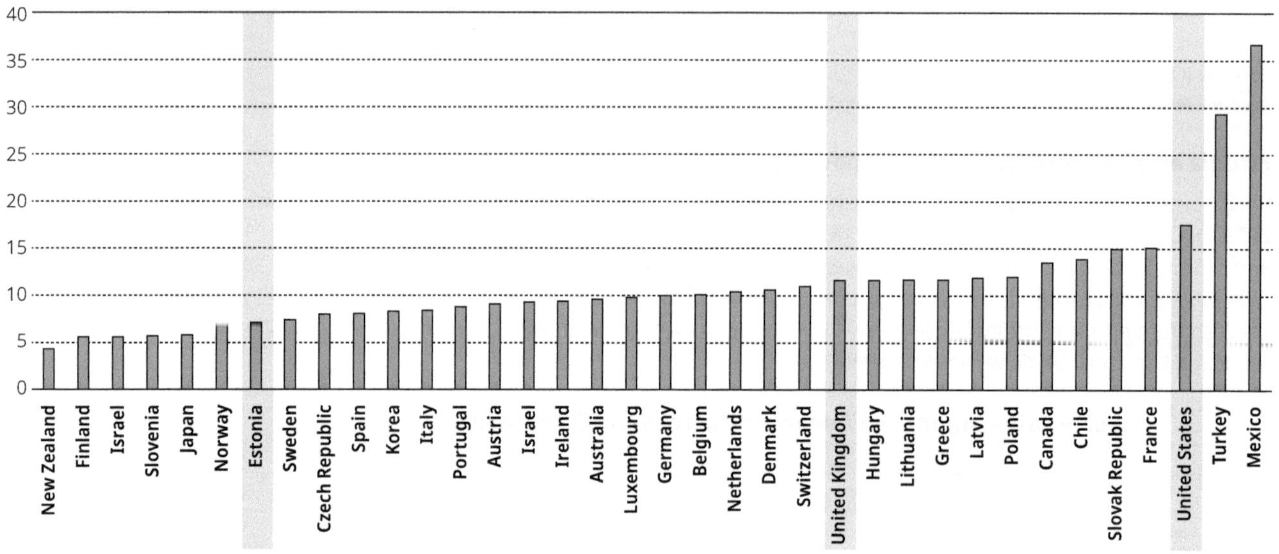

Source: (OECD, 2019[10]) Infant mortality rates (indicator). https://doi.org/10.1787/83dea506-en

StatLink https://doi.org/10.1787/888934110353

England and Estonia have integrated early learning systems

Both England and Estonia have relatively comprehensive early childhood education and care (ECEC) systems in place. Each achieves high take-up rates across socio-economic groups, and are focused on children's holistic development. Both countries operate integrated ECEC systems, where responsibility for ECEC policies largely lies with the education department or ministry, rather than being divided amongst two or more agencies.

The United States, however, operates under a split system. Responsibility for ECEC lies with the Department for Health and Human Services while responsibility for schooling lies with the Department of Education. While responsibility for children's early years in the United States is devolved to state and regional levels, the federal government nonetheless provides grants to states for ECEC provision and funds programmes targeting at-risk children, such as Head Start. However, there is no overall national policy or requirements on states regarding provision, quality or affordability, leading to wide variability in access and affordability across and within states.

Between 2005 and 2017, across OECD countries, the average enrolment of 3-5 year-olds in education rose from 76% to 86% (OECD, 2019). The most significant recent growth in ECEC participation has been among children under three. Increases in ECEC participation over recent decades are strongly correlated to increases in women's labour market participation.

ECEC participation rates are higher in the United Kingdom and Estonia than in the United States. In 2017, 100% of three-year-olds in the United Kingdom participated in ECEC, compared to 91% in Estonia, 42% in the United States and 79% on average across

OECD countries (OECD, 2019). The United Kingdom also achieves universal participation among four-year-olds, while Estonia's rate is 92% and the United States 66%. The OECD average participation rate for four-year-olds is 88%.

OECD countries have used a range of policy levers to increase ECEC participation rates. These include the provision of free ECEC; targeted provision and subsidies for some population groups, usually disadvantaged children; and the extension of compulsory education to younger age levels. A recent example in the United Kingdom has been the targeted support for two-year-olds from disadvantaged families that was put in place in 2013, achieving relatively high take-up rates among the target group (Department for Education, 2019). Some of the children sampled for IELS will have been beneficiaries of this targeted support.

EDUCATION SYSTEM PERFORMANCE

Estonia's education system performs at the highest level, but all three are strong performers

Estonia is one of the best-performing countries in PISA. Estonia was the highest-performing OECD country in reading and science in PISA 2018, and was third in mathematics after Japan and Korea. Estonia has reached this position through steady improvements over successive PISA cycles.

The United Kingdom sits above the OECD mean for these three key competency areas. In PISA 2018, the United Kingdom had increased in the proportion of top performers for reading, among both girls and boys, as part of its gradual improvement over time.

In PISA 2018, the United States performed at a similar level to the United Kingdom for reading and science, but at a significantly lower level in mathematics, below the OECD mean. The United States has remained at similar levels of performance since it participated in the first PISA assessment in 2000.

As with most countries that achieve at the highest level, Estonia also achieves high equity amongst students from different socio-economic groups, as shown in Figure 3.7. Disadvantaged students in the United Kingdom achieved higher scores in 2018 than in previous cycles, whereas the performance gap between advantaged and disadvantaged students has remained constant in the United States.

Figure 3.7 **Strength of the socio-economic gradient and reading performance**

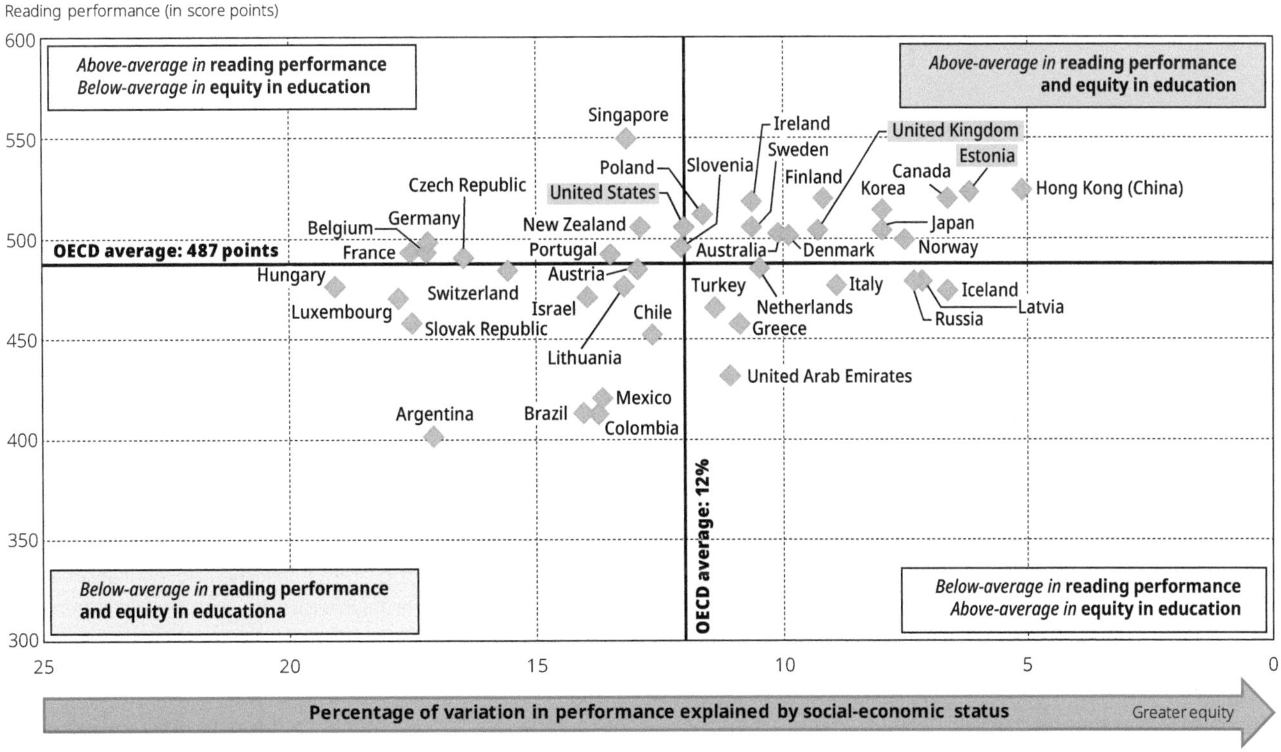

Source: (OECD, 2018[11]), PISA 2018 Database, Table 11.B1.2.3, http://www.oecd.org/pisa/data/2018database/

StatLink https://doi.org/10.1787/888934037184

Estonian mothers are more highly educated than mothers in the United States or England

Mothers' education levels correlate positively with children's early learning outcomes in many studies on children's early years (Shuey et al., 2018). While parents' education is often included in measures of socio-economic status, parental education tends to be more strongly associated with children's early outcomes than household income (Sylva et al, 2008[14]). Parents' education levels are also correlated to the activities parents do with their children, such as reading from books and talking with them. The latter are both key facets of children's home learning environments. Parental education also influences decisions about children's participation in ECEC (Shuey and Kankaraš 2018[15]).

Women in all three participating countries are more highly educated than men, although the gender gap is wider in Estonia than in the United Kingdom or the United States. The proportion of 25-34 year-old women with tertiary education[6] is very similar in all three countries, at 54%, sitting above the OECD mean of 51% (Figure 3.8).

Figure 3.8 Proportion of men and women with tertiary education across OECD countries

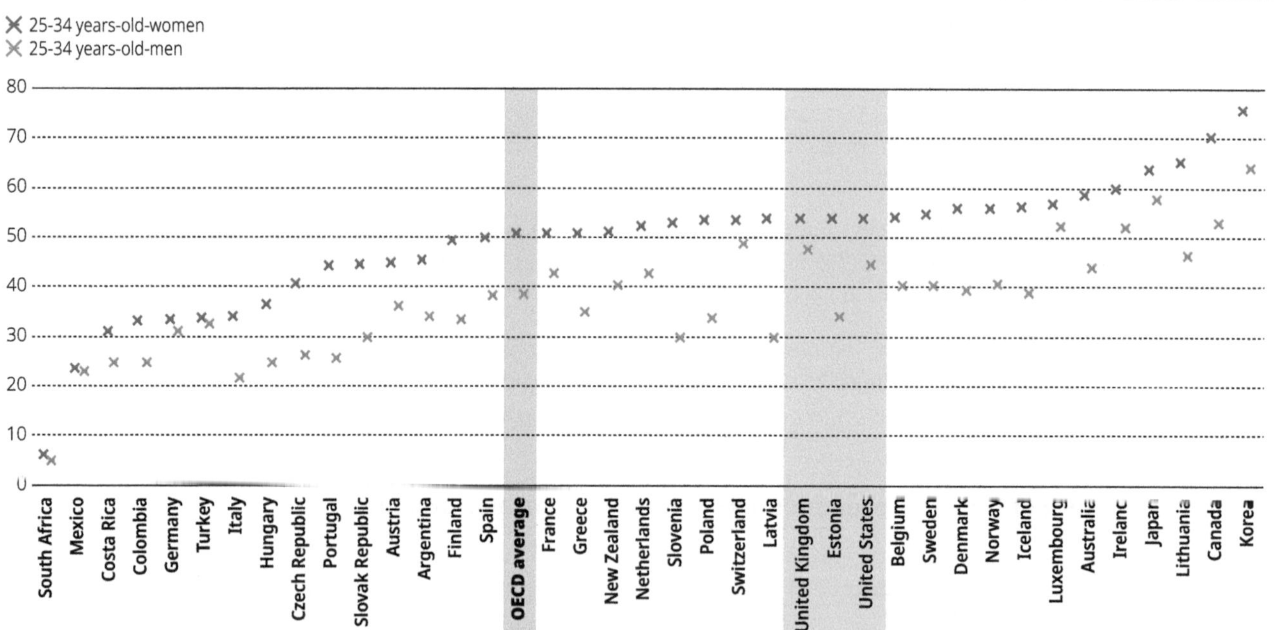

Source: (OECD, 2019[12]), Population with tertiary education (indicator). https://doi.org/10.1787/0b8f90e9-en, (accessed on 20 October 2019).

StatLink https://doi.org/10.1787/888934110372

In the IELS sample, 53% of the mothers in Estonia had at least a bachelor's degree, compared to 40% in England and 39% in the United States.[7]

CONCLUSIONS

The three countries in this study each have distinct contexts and systems for supporting children and their families in the early years. Estonia and the United States differ immensely in size, wealth, equity, family and child policies and, to a lesser extent, education performance. England often occupies the middle ground being closer to Estonia on child and family policies and closer to the United States on demographic diversity. Nonetheless, each of the three countries has relatively well-developed education systems, equipping their students and young people with the skills they need.

Each new cohort of parents and children, however, can differ from previous cohorts. The lives of families and of young children can alter in response to changes such as family structures, gender roles, employment patterns, income and education levels, and housing and neighbourhood factors. These all affect the nature and extent of parental interactions with their children, and children's engagement in learning at and outside of school. As a result, learning and education outcomes at a country level can and do change over time.

By paying attention to children's early learning, countries can make immense improvements to the outcomes for individual children and their families, as well as using an effective and cost-efficient means to lift the performance of their education systems overall. To achieve such improvements, countries need reliable, valid and comparable data. This enables countries to see what is possible in children's early learning, monitor progress at a system-level over time and take action to improve children's outcomes.

The next three chapters set out the findings from this study on children's early learning and development. These chapters cover the findings in each of the three early learning domains covered by the study: social-emotional skills, self-regulation and cognitive skills. The findings highlight the early learning of different groups of children as well as the factors that are associated with positive early learning.

References

Department of Work and Pensions, UK Government (2019), *Table 4.5db: Percentage of cHouseholds below average income: 1994/95 to 2017/18*, UK Government, www.gov.uk/government/statistics/households-below-average-income-199495-to-201718 (accessed on October 15 2019). [8]

Federal Interagency Forum on Child and Family Statistics (2018), *America's Children in Brief: Key National Indicators of Well-Being, 2018*, Federal Interagency Forum on Child and Family Statistics, www.childstats.gov/pdf/ac2018/ac_18.pdf (accessed on 14 February 2019). [2]

OECD (2020), *Population (indicator)*, https://doi.org/10.1787/0b8f90e9-en (accessed on 2020 February 2020). [1]

OECD (2019), *Education at a Glance 2019: OECD Indicators*, OECD Publishing, Paris, https://doi.org/10.1787/f8d7880d-en. [13]

OECD (2019), *Income inequality (indicator)*, https://doi.org/10.1787/459aa7f1-en (accessed on 15 October 2019). [6]

OECD (2019), *Infant mortality rates (indicator)*, https://doi.org/10.1787/83dea506-en (accessed on 26 October 2019). [10]

OECD (2019), *Level of GDP per capita and productivity*, https://stats.oecd.org/Index.aspx?DataSetCode=PDB_L (accessed on 20 October 2019). [5]

OECD (2019), *Poverty rate (indicator)*, https://doi.org/10.1787/0fe1315d-en (accessed on 10 October 2019). [7]

OECD (2019), *Tertiary graduation rate (indicator)*, https://doi.org/10.1787/15c523d3-en (accessed on 20 October 2019). [12]

OECD (2019), *Treating all children equally? Why policies should adapt to evolving family realities*, www.oecd.org/els/family/child-well-being/Treating-all-children-equally-Policy-brief-2019.pdf (accessed on 15 October 2019). [4]

OECD (2018), *PISA 2018 Database, Table 11.B1.2.3* www.oecd.org/pisa/data/2018database/. [11]

Shuey, E. and M. Kankaraš (2018), *"The Power and Promise of Early Learning", OECD Education Working Papers*, No. 186, OECD Publishing, Paris, https://dx.doi.org/10.1787/f9b2e53f-en. [15]

Statistics Estonia (2019), *Statistical Database*, Statistics Estonia website, http://andmebaas.stat.ee/Index.aspx?lang=en&SubSessionId=da2e6b42-6b36-4f33-87cc-e7e993bae966&themetreeid=6 (accessed on 10 April 2019). [3]

Sylva, K. et al. (2008), *Final report from the primary phase: Pre-school, school and family influences on children's development during Key Stage 2 (7-11) Publication Details*, http://ro.uow.edu.au/sspapers/1807 (accessed on 4 February 2020). [14]

UNICEF (2018), *Breastfeeding a Mother's Gift for Every Child*, www.unicef.org/publications/files/UNICEF_Breastfeeding_A_Mothers_Gift_for_Every_Child.pdf. [9]

Notes

1. In some cases, data for the United Kingdom is used rather than for England, where information on England has not been accessible.

2. Note that England represents 84% of the total population of the United Kingdom (Office for National Statistics, 2019).

3. The term "social parent" refers to an adult who is living in an informal arrangement with a child's parent. Social siblings refer to the children of a child's social parent.

4. GDP per capita is a measure of a country's economic output that accounts for its number of people. It divides the country's gross domestic product by its total population, providing an indicator of a country's standard of living.

5. The child relative income poverty rate is defined as the percentage of children (0-17 years) with an equivalised household disposable income (i.e. an income after taxes and transfers adjusted for household size) below the poverty threshold. The poverty threshold is 50% of the median disposable income in each country.

6. Tertiary education is defined as Level 5 and above on the International Standard Classification of Education (ISCED), i.e. generally at bachelor's degree level and above.

7. Insufficient responses were received on fathers' educational qualifications to report these.

Social-emotional skills

This chapter presents findings on the social-emotional skills of five-year-olds in England, Estonia and the United States. It shows the differences in social-emotional scores across multiple subgroups of children, considering their individual and family characteristics, as well as their home learning environments. This is based on a direct assessment of children's skills and reports from the children's parents and teachers.

Children's social-emotional development influences the extent to which they can play well with other children, make friends and thrive in group settings, such as in early childhood education and care (ECEC) or school. It also influences how well they are able to learn a range of other skills.

The International Early Learning and Child Well-being Study (IELS) found variations in children's social-emotional learning across the three countries taking part, as well as within countries among different groups of children. These are largely consistent with findings for children's self-regulation and cognitive skills, as outlined in the following chapters, although there are distinct findings on the social-emotional learning of five-year-olds in the three countries.

Children in Estonia scored more highly across almost all of the social-emotional skills assessed than those in the other two countries. Across all three countries, girls scored more highly than boys in each aspect of social-emotional learning. Children from higher socio-economic backgrounds were also rated as having higher social-emotional skills than children from disadvantaged homes, also in all three countries.

Children from immigrant backgrounds[1] were reported by their teachers to have lower levels of prosocial behaviour and trust than other children, as well as lower levels of disruptive behaviour. Similar results were reported by teachers for children who spoke a different language at home from that used in the ECEC centre or school they attended.

Having experienced learning or social, emotional or behavioral difficulties was also associated with lower levels of social-emotional development. Learning difficulties were associated with lower scores for emotional identification, emotion attribution, prosocial behaviour and trust. Social, emotional or behavioural difficulties were linked to lower scores for all social-emotional skills.

The activities that parents undertake with their children are significantly associated with their children's social-emotional development. This includes engaging in back-and-forth conversations, reading to their children regularly, role-playing, being involved in their children's ECEC centre or school and taking their children to special activities such as dance and swimming.

This chapter describes:

- the critical importance of children's social-emotional skills for their development, later outcomes and well-being
- the findings of the study in relation to children's social-emotional skills.

These findings are based on analysis of representative samples of just under 7 000 five-year-olds in England, Estonia and the United States.

SOCIAL-EMOTIONAL SKILLS ARE CRITICAL FOR CHILDREN'S DEVELOPMENT AND WELL-BEING

The development of children's social-emotional skills is inextricably linked to their cognitive development and to their sense of overall well-being (Shuey and Kankaraš, 2018[1]). Indeed, developments in neuroscience have shown that the neural circuits involved in the regulation of emotions overlap with those associated with cognitive processing (Bush, Luu and Posner, 2000[2]; Davidson et al., 2002[3]; Posner and Rothbart, 2000[4]). Thus, cognitive development can be impeded when emotions are not well regulated. For instance, children who are not in control of their emotions are more prone to outbursts, inattention and rapid retreats from stressful situations (Garber and Dodge, 1991[5]).

Moreover, early social experiences are linked to emotional development and the construction of critical foundational capacities (Scientific Council on the Developing Child, 2004[6]). Rich social interactions during the early years coupled with secure attachments to parents and responsive caregivers prepare children to develop social-emotional skills during adolescence and adulthood, even if their later environments are not as nurturing. Conversely, children deprived of appropriate sensory, emotional, and social experiences during their early years are more likely to behave disruptively, with detrimental effects on their cognitive development (Shonkoff and Phillips, 2000[7]).

EARLY SOCIAL-EMOTIONAL SKILLS ARE PREDICTIVE OF A RANGE OF LATER OUTCOMES

Early self-control and prosocial behaviour are associated with later educational attainment, socio-economic status, income and unemployment. Social-emotional skills that are learned during childhood are linked to educational achievement even after controlling for early literacy and numeracy (Duncan et al., 2007[8]). Skills such as self-control and the ability to delay gratification are strongly associated with educational attainment, socio-economic status and income later in life (Schoon et al., 2015[9]).

Furthermore, early prosocial behaviour at the age of 8 has shown to be as important as early cognitive ability in predicting education attainment at the age of 30 (Schoon et al., 2015[9]) as well as in shaping attainment in adolescence and adulthood (Caprara et al., 2000[10]).

Early social-emotional skills help children to build and maintain close relationships with their parents and other family members, as well as make positive social connections outside the family. These skills help children to play and to form early friendships with other children. In turn, these social interactions build children's ability to regulate their emotions and behaviours, their language skills and their sense of well-being (Shuey and Kankaraš, 2018[1]).

In adulthood, early social-emotional skills are one of the strongest predictors of life satisfaction, general well-being and mental health. Findings from the British Cohort Study and National Child Development Study revealed that children's emotional health was the strongest predictor of adult life satisfaction at all ages, even more than family economic resources, family psychosocial resources and children's cognitive ability (Flèche, Lekfuangfu and Clark, 2019[11]). Furthermore, early emotional well-being is linked with better mental health in later life, and emotional difficulties among five-year-olds are predictors of midlife psychological disorders such as anxiety and depression (Rutter, Kim-Cohen and Maughan, 2006[12]; Buchanan, Flouri and Brinke, 2002[13]).

Early empathy, trust and prosocial behaviour are associated with a lower likelihood of involvement in delinquency, violence and other crime in adulthood. In particular children with low levels of empathy are more at risk of psychopathology as adults than other children (Fontaine et al., 2011[14]).

The study focuses on children's skills in recognising and regulating emotions as well as expressing positive social behaviour

IELS focused on children's skills in recognising and regulating emotions and actions as well as understanding the emotions of others. Furthermore, IELS emphasised the behavioural aspects of social-emotional skills and included the expression of positive social behaviour, through co-operation and the lack of disruptive behaviour. A core component of empathy is children's recognition of others' emotions (emotion identification) and their emotional responsiveness to the feelings of others (emotion attribution) (Strayer, 1987[15]; Strayer, 1993[16]). Prosocial behaviour is the combination of the expression of positive social behaviour (express) and conformity with teachers' or parents' expectations (comply) (Hogan, Scott and Bauer, 1992[17]). Both emotion identification and emotion attribution act as precursors to engaging in prosocial behaviour in response to another person's emotional state.

Trust was another central aspect of IELS: the child's expectations that others will be protective and benevolent (responsive, kind), which overlaps with security of attachment (Bowlby, 1969[18]). By preschool, children generalise their expectations of responsiveness from parents to other children and other adults. Thus, trusting (or securely attached) five-year-olds expect classmates to be reasonable and co-operative and teachers to be protective and benevolent (Sroufe, 2005[19]). Just as there are various ways to be insecure, there are multiple ways to be mistrustful. Mistrustful children might be overly wary or fearful of peers or adults, reluctant to engage with others, or be needy and dependent since they do not trust others to always be responsive and supportive.

Children participating in IELS responded to hypothetical (story) scenarios designed to elicit empathy. The narrated stories consisted of brief vignettes with cartoon-like characters (Figure 4.1). The measurement of empathy included both how well children could recognise the emotions of the characters in the stories and how the child felt and why in response to the situations portrayed within each story. The child interacted with the stories via an electronic tablet, with one-to-one support from a trained study administrator.

In addition, both parents and teachers provided information about children's social-emotional skills. By collecting data from parents and teachers as well as the direct assessment, IELS aimed to provide a comprehensive assessment of early social-emotional skills. Parents and teachers responded to questions relating to children's empathy, trust and their prosocial and disruptive behaviour, including emotional control. Reports of disruptive behaviour were inverted, so that non-disruptive rather than disruptive behaviour is reported.

4

Figure 4.1 **Children were asked how characters in the IELS stories were feeling**

OVERALL FINDINGS

Children in Estonia identify others' emotions more accurately and have stronger prosocial behaviour than children in England or the United States, but are more disruptive

A higher proportion of children in Estonia accurately identified others' emotions in the direct assessment than children in England or the United States. In addition, teachers reported higher prosocial skills among children in Estonia than reported by teachers in the other two countries. In contrast, however, teachers in Estonia also reported children in Estonia as more disruptive than reported by teachers in the other two countries. There were no significant differences across the three countries in the mean scores for emotion attribution and trust.

Findings for each of the three countries on the social-emotional skills measured by this study are set out in Table 4.1.

Table 4.1 **Mean scores in social-emotional skills, by country**

	Emotion identification	Emotion attribution	Prosocial behaviour	Trust	Non-disruptive behaviour
Estonia	511	500	511	503	470
England	497	500	495	504	515
United States	493	500	494	493	515

Figure 4.2 shows the distribution of scores for emotion identification, emotion attribution, prosocial behaviour, trust and non-disruptive behaviour, by country. Children in England and the United States demonstrated similar skill levels in identifying others' emotions, whereas a greater proportion of children in Estonia scored at the upper end of the skill distribution. While the average score was the same for emotion attribution in each country, the scores for children in Estonia were more widely spread than in England or the United States. In prosocial skills, the three countries had similar proportions of children at the lower skill levels but Estonia had more children scoring at the upper levels of the skill distribution. While there were no significant differences in the country means for trust, a higher percentage of children in England and Estonia were reported to have very high levels of trust than reported in the United States. For non-disruptive behaviour, England and the United States again demonstrated a similar distribution across scores, whereas a higher proportion of children in Estonia were reported to have lower levels of non-disruptive behaviour.

Figure 4.2 **Distribution of children's social-emotional skills, by country**

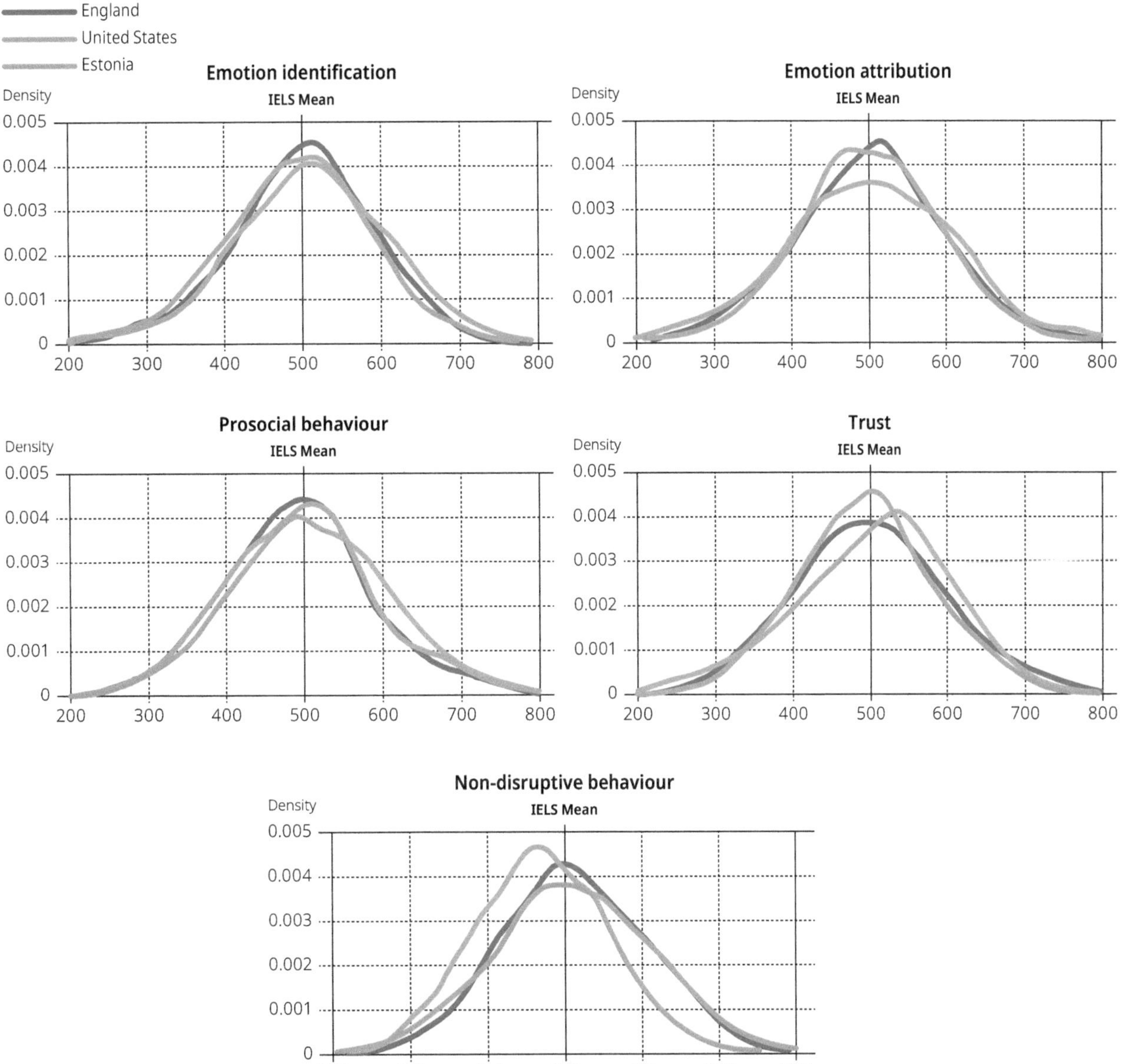

Note: Distribution produced using the first plausible value only.

Children's social-emotional skills increase with age

As expected, children's social-emotional skills develop as they mature. The largest differences based on age in months related to emotion identification and emotion attribution, which are set out in Figure 4.3. Differences based on age were smaller for prosocial and non-disruptive behaviour, and even smaller for trust. The increases in scores relating to children's age in months were similar between boys and girls as well as between children from high and low socio-economic groups.

Girls have more developed social-emotional skills than boys

There was a significant gender difference in favour of girls for each of the five measures of children's social-emotional skills, in all three countries (Figure 4.4). The largest gender difference was for prosocial behaviour, followed by emotion identification and non-disruptive behaviour. Among the three countries, the largest gender differences were found in Estonia and the smallest in the United States. Gender differences were similar across socio-economic groups.

Figure 4.3 **Social-emotion skills by age in months, by country**

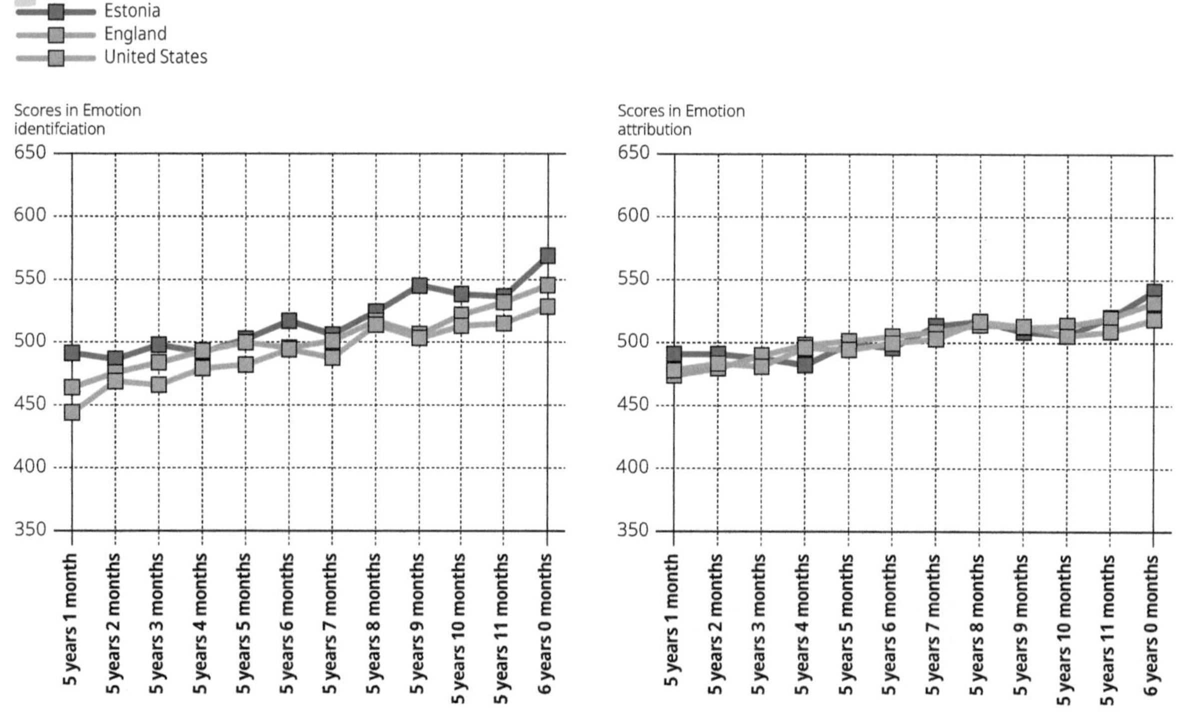

StatLink https://doi.org/10.1787/888934110410

Figure 4.4 **Social-emotional scores, by gender**

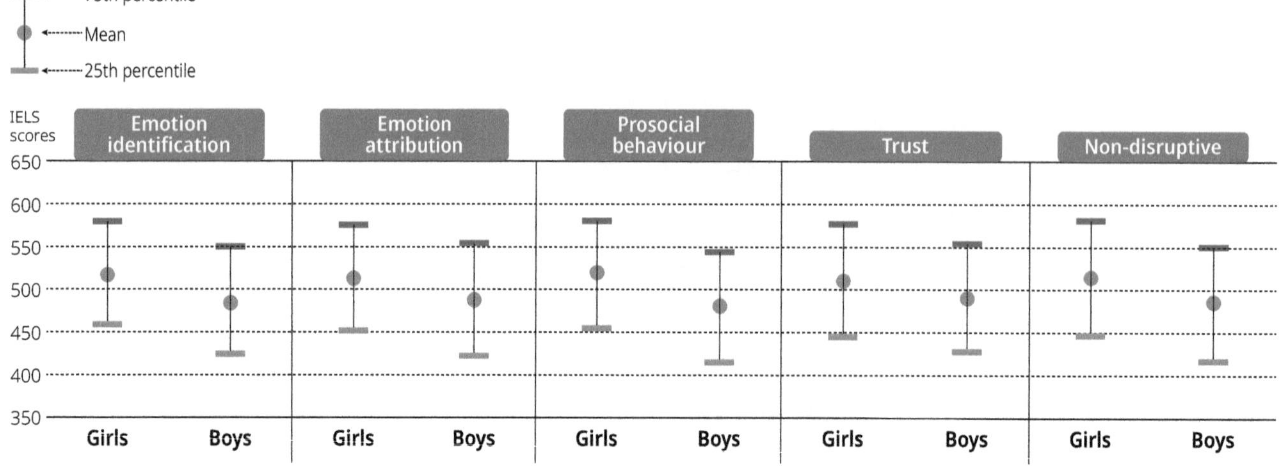

Note: The gender differences in mean, 25th percentile, and 75th percentile scores are statistically significant.
StatLink https://doi.org/10.1787/888934110429

Both parents and teachers reported girls as having higher social-emotional skills than boys, although teachers reported larger gender differences than parents. At the same time, parents' views of their children's social-emotional skills were more positive than the reports from teachers, for both boys and girls, and particularly for empathy. Parent and teacher responses to specific questions on children's social-emotional development are provided in Figure 4.5.

Figure 4.5 **Social-emotional development as reported by parents and teachers, by gender**

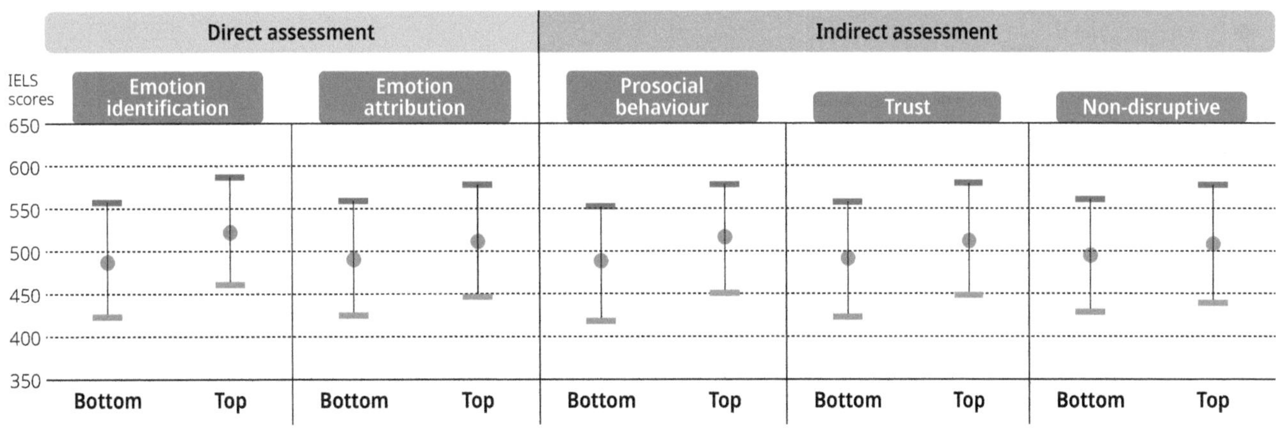

Note: The figure is comparing the same children rated by their teachers and parents.

StatLink https://doi.org/10.1787/888934110448

Children from higher socio-economic backgrounds have more developed social-emotional skills than their less advantaged peers

There were positive associations between socio-economic background and children's scores in both the direct assessments of empathy and teachers' reports of children's social-emotional skills (Figure 4.6). The size of these associations were similar across the three countries for emotion identification, prosocial behaviour, trust and non-disruptive behaviour. The relationship between socio-economic background and emotion attribution was smaller in Estonia in comparison with England, and similar to that in the United States.

Figure 4.6 **Children's social-emotional skills, by socio-economic status**

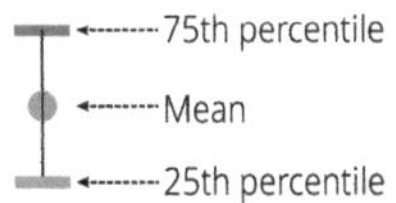

Note: The differences between the top and bottom quartile of SES are statistically significant.

StatLink https://doi.org/10.1787/888934110467

The largest difference associated with children's socio-economic background was in emotion identification and the least in non-disruptive behaviour. The correlations between socio-economic status and disruptive behaviour were relatively small across all three countries, and only statistically significant in England.

Parents and teachers were more likely to report children from higher socio-economic groups as having stronger social-emotional skills than children from lower socio-economic groups (Figure 4.7). Among parents, these reported differences were greater for empathy than for emotional control.

Figure 4.7 **Social-emotional development as reported by parents and teachers, by socio-economic status**

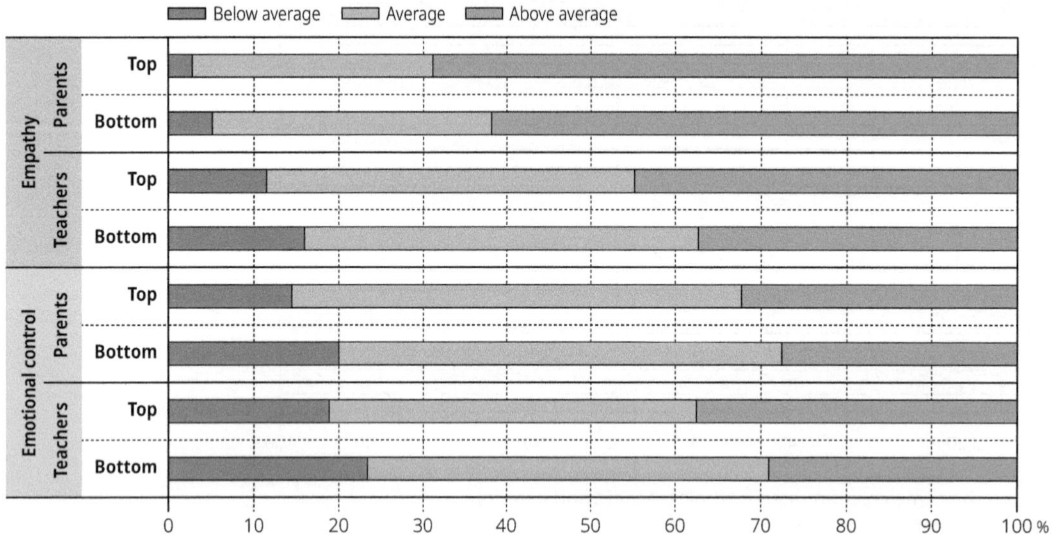

Note: The figure is comparing the same children rated by their teachers and parents.

StatLink https://doi.org/10.1787/888934110486

Children with an immigrant background have lower levels of trust and prosocial behaviour than other children, but are less disruptive

Approximately 12% of children in the study across the three countries had an immigrant background. The relationships between having an immigrant background and social-emotional development at an individual country level were not significant, once socio-economic status and home language were taken into account. However, when the findings from the three countries were combined, the study found having an immigrant background was associated with lower trust and prosocial behaviour, as well as lower levels of disruptive behaviour, as shown in Figure 4.8.

Figure 4.8 **Social-emotional scores, by immigrant background**

Score-point differences between children with an immigrant background and those without, before and after accounting for socio-economic status and home language

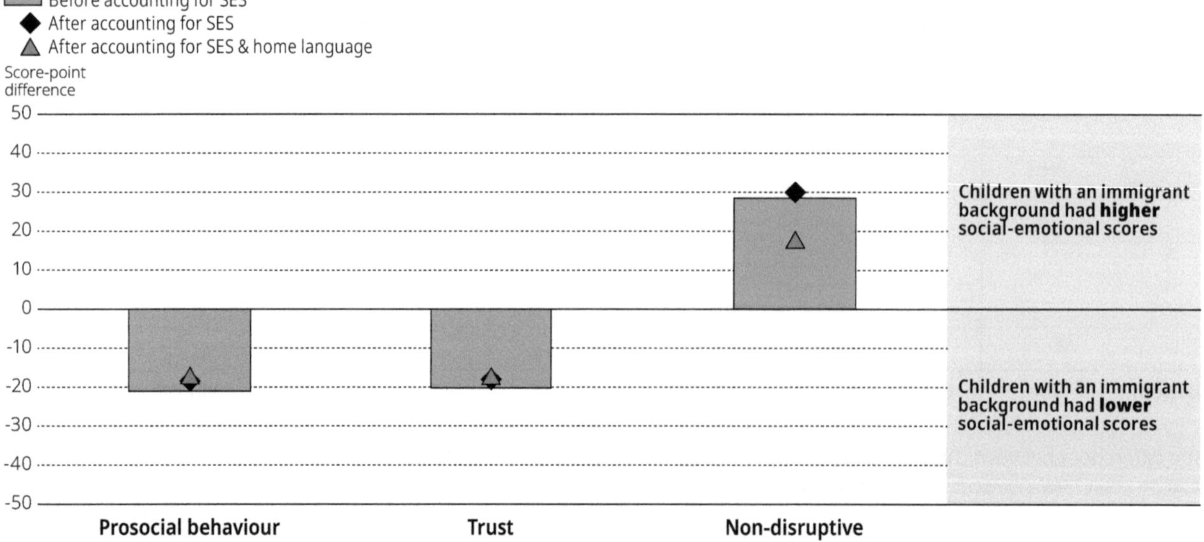

Note: All differences are statistically significant.

StatLink https://doi.org/10.1787/888934110505

Parents with an immigrant background rated their children's social-emotional skills at similar levels to other parents. Both groups of parents had more positive views of their children's empathy skills than their children's levels of emotional control (Figure 4.9).

Figure 4.9 **Social-emotional development as reported by parents and teachers, by immigrant background**

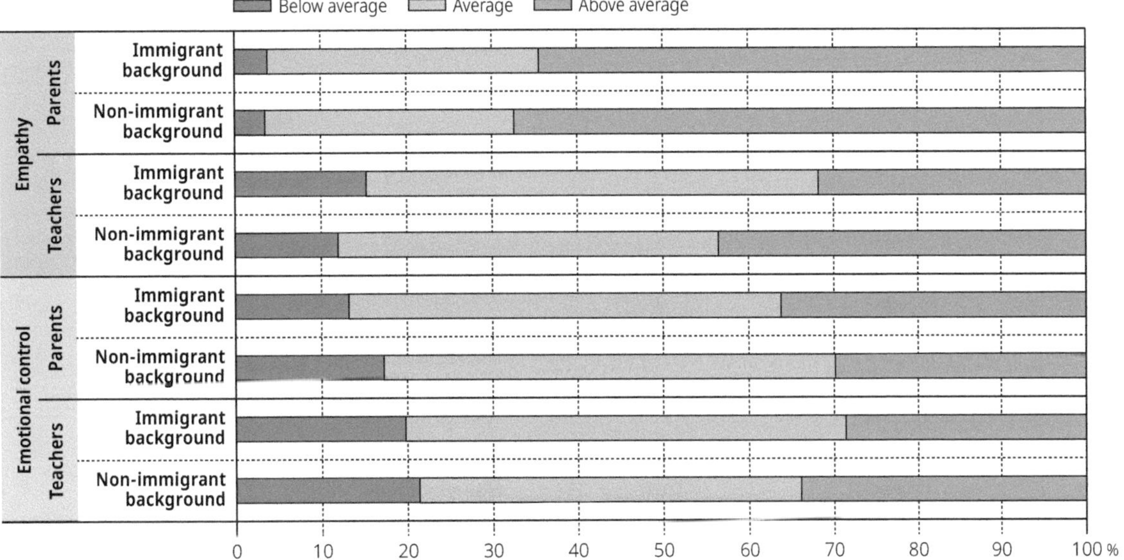

Note: The figure is comparing the same children rated by their teachers and parents.
StatLink https://doi.org/10.1787/888934110524

Children with a different home language from their ECEC centre or school are less disruptive than other children

Parents of children in the study were also asked to identify whether one or both parents spoke a language at home that was different from the language of the ECEC centre or school that the child attends.[2] Across the three countries, 13% of children in this study had a different home language.

The direct assessments were carried out in English in England and in the United States, and in Estonian or Russian in Estonia.

The study did not find significant differences at an individual country level between children who had a different home language from their ECEC centre or school and other children. When the findings from each country are combined, children with a different home language to their ECEC centre or school had lower scores for emotion attribution in the direct assessment and were reported by teachers to have lower levels of prosocial behaviour and trust than other children. Similar to children with an immigrant background, children with a different home language were reported by their teachers as being less disruptive than other children, as illustrated in Figure 4.10.

Parents of children who had a different home language from the language of their child's ECEC centre or school had a similar view of their children's empathy skills and a slightly more positive view of their children's emotional control to other parents. Both groups of parents had more positive views of their children's empathy skills than teachers, but similar view on their children's levels of emotional control (Figure 4.11).

Learning and behavioural difficulties are negatively associated with social-emotional learning

Parents also provided information on whether their child was premature or had a low birthweight[3], learning difficulties (e.g. speech or language delay, intellectual disability) or social, emotional or behavioural difficulties. Across the three countries, the mean percentage of children with at least one of these challenges was 24%, with a mean of 9% having experienced low birthweight or who had been premature, 11% having experienced learning difficulties and 10% having experienced social, emotional or behavioural difficulties. On average across countries, 5% of children had experienced two of these challenges and 1%, on average, experienced all three.

Overall, parents in England and Estonia reported fewer children with these challenges than parents in the United States. Parents in Estonia reported the smallest proportion of premature and low birth weight children while parents in England reported the smallest proportion of children with behavioural difficulties.

Figure 4.10 **Social-emotional scores, by home language**

Score-point differences between children with at least one parent who speaks a language other than the assessment language at home and children with parent(s) who mainly speak the assessment language at home

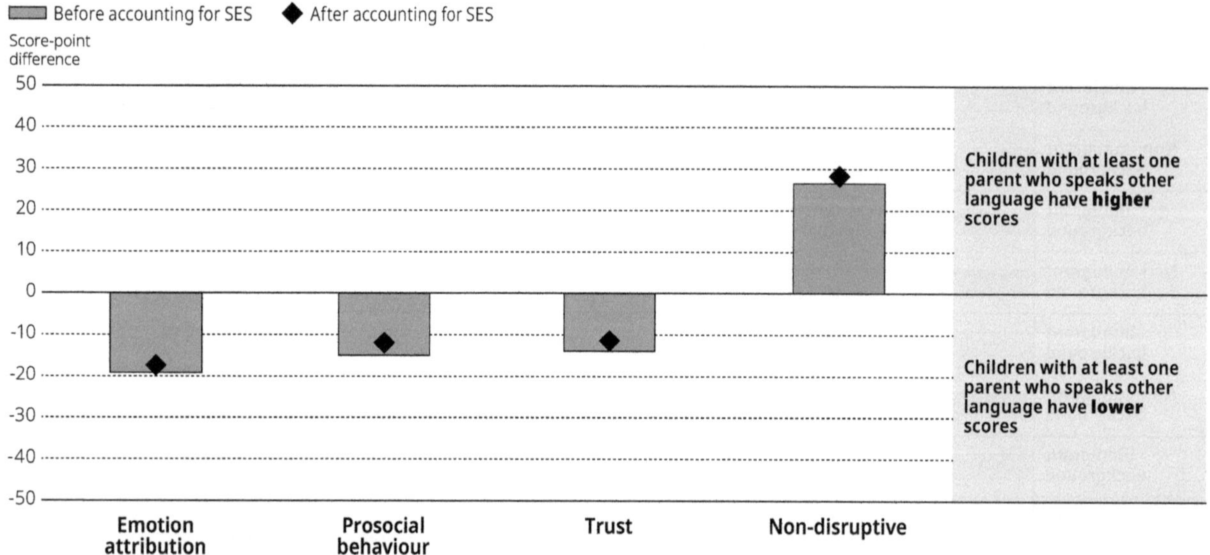

Note: All differences are statistically significant.

StatLink https://doi.org/10.1787/888934110543

Figure 4.11 **Social-emotional development as reported by parents and teachers, by home language**

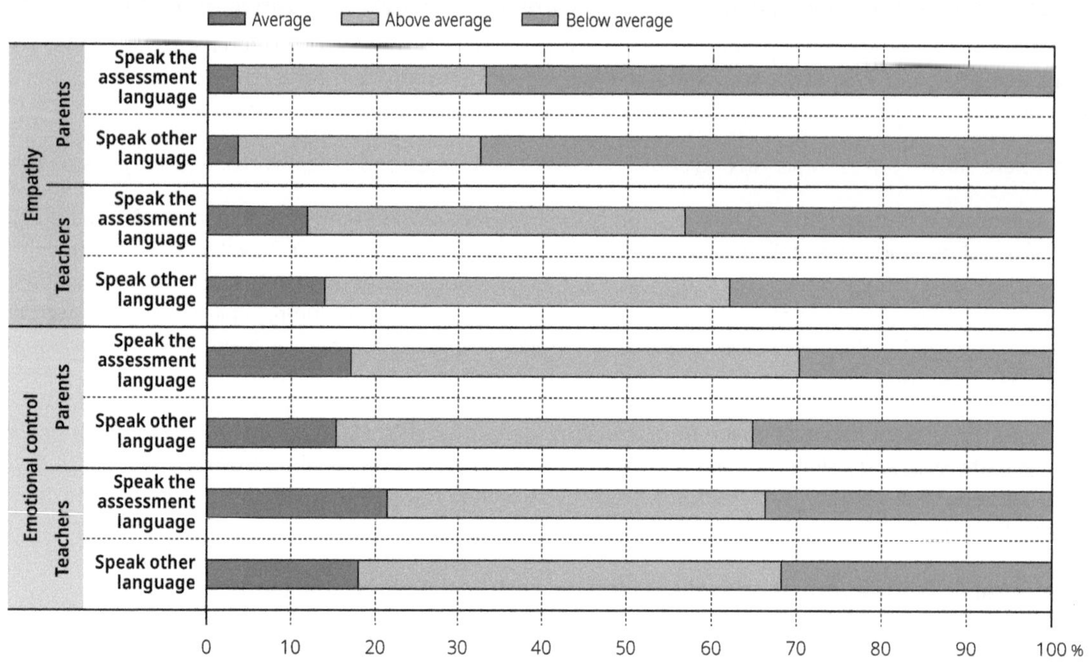

Note: The figure is comparing the same children rated by their teachers and parents.

StatLink https://doi.org/10.1787/888934110562

There was no significant gender difference in the proportion of children who had been premature or who had a low birth weight. Boys were twice as likely as girls to be reported by their parents as having learning difficulties and a similar ratio of boys to girls were reported by their parents as having behavioural difficulties. Similarly, children from low socio-economic backgrounds were a little more than twice as likely to be reported by their parents as having learning difficulties or social, emotional or behavioural difficulties.

Premature birth and low birthweight had the smallest association with children's social-emotional scores, as illustrated in Figure 4.12. Learning difficulties were most negatively associated with children's ability to identify others' emotions, prosocial behaviour and trust. Social, emotional or behavioural difficulties were negatively associated with all five dimensions of children's social-emotional skills, particularly for reported levels of prosocial and non-disruptive behaviour. Children who were premature or had a low birthweight and children who had learning difficulties were not reported by their teachers as more disruptive than other children (Figure 4.12).

Figure 4.12 **Association between early difficulties and social-emotional scores**

Score-point differences between children who have and have not experienced an early difficulty, before and after accounting for socio-economic status

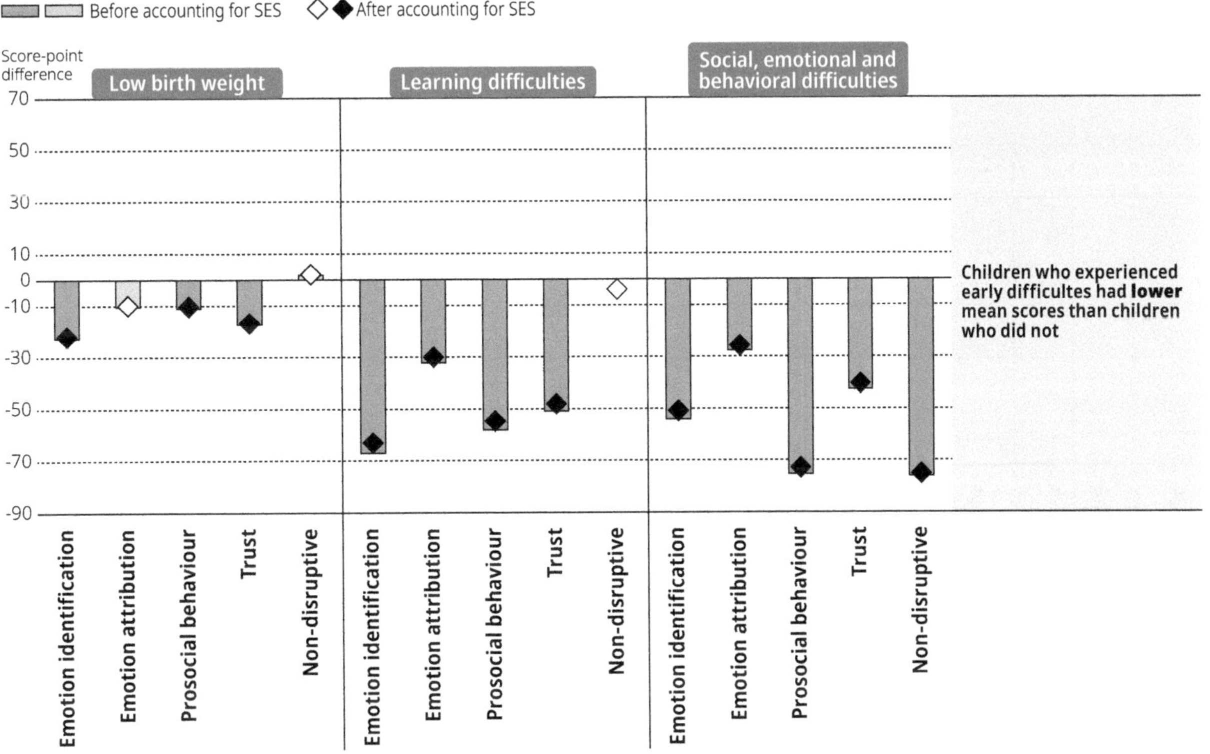

Note: Darker coloured markers indicate that the difference is statistically significant.

StatLink https://doi.org/10.1787/888934110581

Parent-child activities are positively associated with children's social-emotional skills

The activities parents undertake with their children and other aspects of the home learning environment are significantly associated with children's social-emotional skills. Children whose parents engage them in back-and-forth conversations about how they feel are more able to accurately identify others' emotions. Children whose parents regularly read books to them and engage them in role-play activities were also found to have more positive social-emotional skills and behaviour (Figure 4.13).

A higher proportion of parents in England (59%) reported that they read to their children 5-7 days a week than parents in Estonia (28%) or the United States (43%). Children from advantaged backgrounds were much more likely to be read to 5-7 days a week (60% on average across the three countries) than children from disadvantaged backgrounds (30%).

Teachers were asked how involved parents were with the ECEC centre or school the child attended, ranging from not involved to slightly, moderately or strongly involved. Teachers in Estonia reported that 80% of parents were moderately or strongly involved, compared to 69% of parents in England and 65% in the United States. More parents from high SES groups (84%) were reported to be involved in their child's ECEC centre or school than parents from low SES groups (67%).

Children whose parents were involved in their ECEC centre or school had stronger empathy and higher ratings for prosocial skills and trust and lower ratings for disruptive behaviour than other children (Figure 4.14).

Figure 4.13 **Social-emotional scores by frequency of being read to by parents**

After accounting for socio-economic status

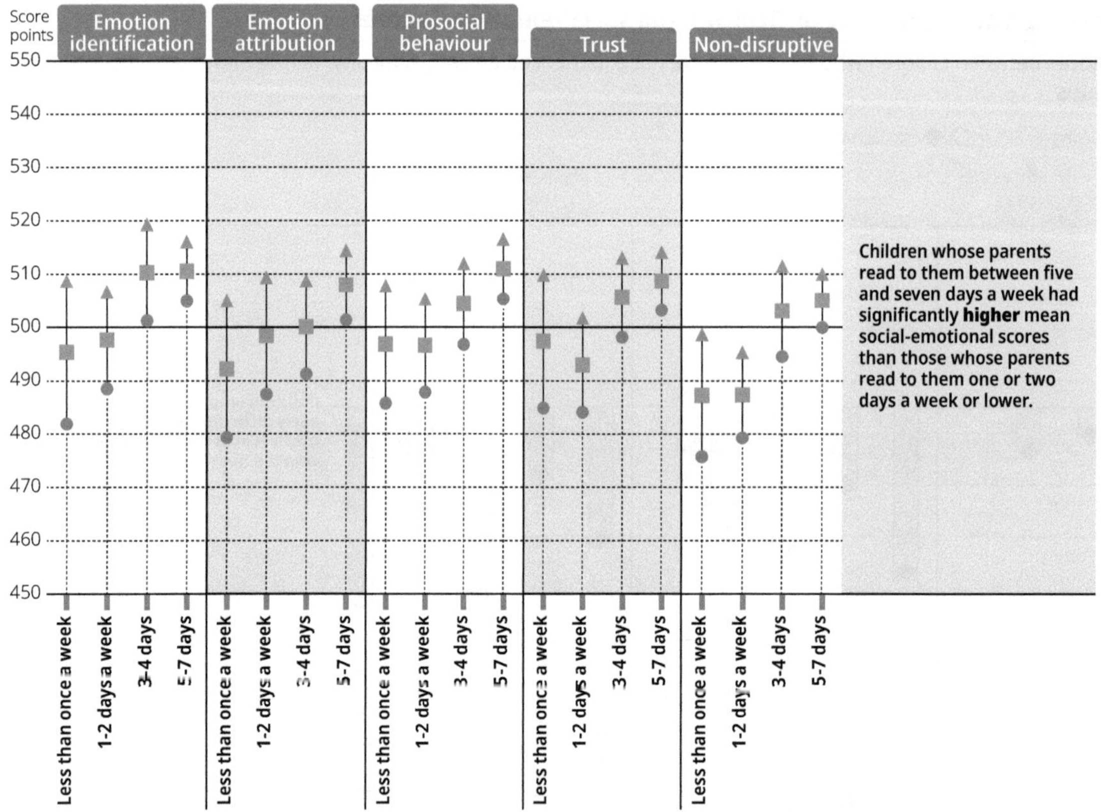

StatLink https://doi.org/10.1787/888934110600

Other elements of children's home environment that were positively associated with their social-emotional skills were having children's books in the home and taking part in special activities such as sports or scouts (Figure 4.15).

Children in Estonia were more likely to attend special activities at least 3 times a week than children in England or the United States. Children in the United States were more likely to never attend or attend less than once a week than children in the other two countries. Boys and girls were, on average, equally likely to be taken to such activities. Children from high socio-economic backgrounds were more likely to attend such activities at least 3 times a week (22%), compared to children from low socio-economic backgrounds (11%).

While parents, in the main, were equally likely to undertake these activities with both their daughters and their sons, parents reported more frequent role-play with girls than with boys.

Mothers' education levels are positively correlated with children's social-emotional skills

Children whose mothers had completed tertiary education[4] had higher scores for social-emotional learning than children whose mothers had not (Figure 4.16). After accounting for socio-economic status, mothers' education levels were significantly correlated with emotion identification, prosocial behaviour and trust.

Parents' with higher levels of education were more likely to engage their children in activities that help children to develop, such as reading to them from books. In addition, studies of children's early development have also found independent positive

effects, particularly of mothers' educational attainment (Sylva et al., 2003[25]). As noted in Chapter 3 on the characteristics of each participating country, Estonian mothers were more likely to have a bachelor degree (53%) than either England (40%) or the United States (39%).

Figure 4.14 **Social-emotional scores by parental involvement in school activities**

After accounting for socio-economic status

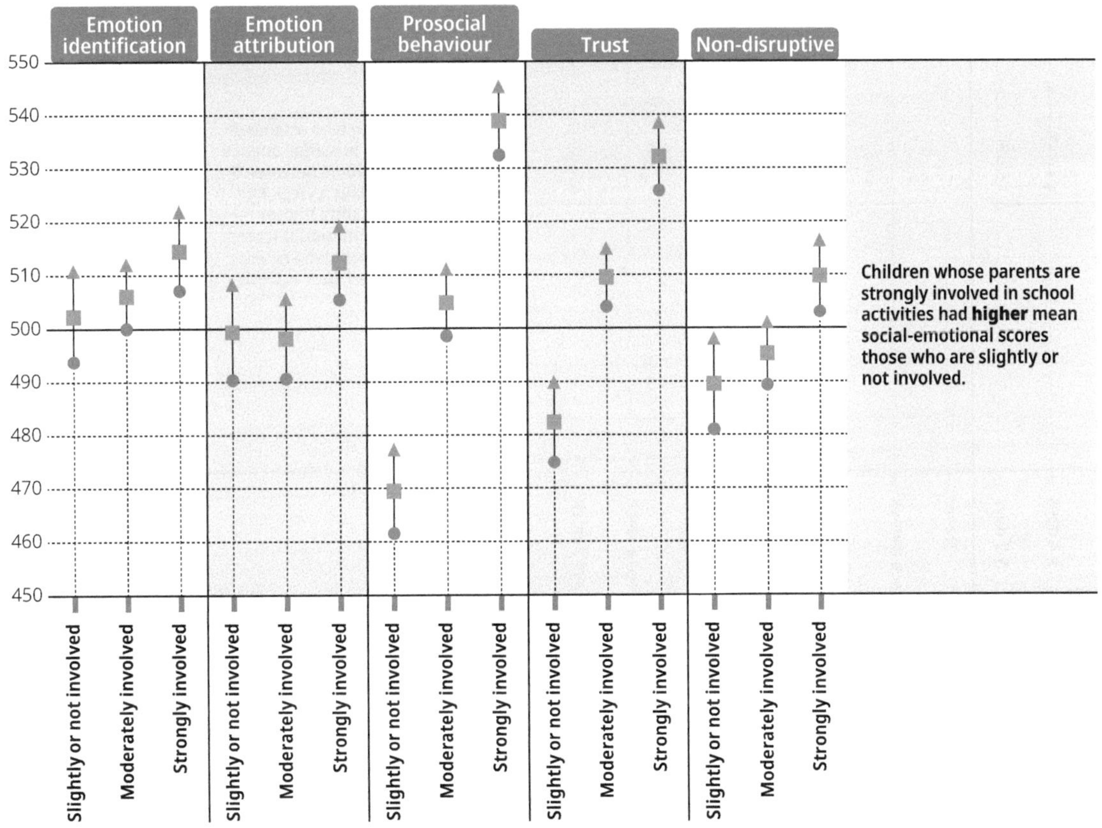

StatLink https://doi.org/10.1787/888934110619

The use of digital devices shows little relationship with children's social-emotional skills

On average across the three participating countries, 83% of children used a digital device at least once a week, with 42% using such devices every day. Only 7% of the children never or hardly ever used digital devices, with 10% using one at least monthly, but not weekly.

Access to digital devices had little association with children's overall social-emotional scores.

There are few associations between household composition and children's social-emotional skills

While children from single-parent households were reported by their teachers to have higher levels of disruptive behaviour in the United States, after accounting for the household's socio-economic status, this was not the case in England or Estonia. There were no differences between children from single-parent and two-parent households for any of the other indicators of social-emotional skills. This was equally the case for boys and for girls.

Children with one or more siblings in England and Estonia were less likely to be disruptive than children without siblings, but there was no such difference in the United States.

Figure 4.15 **Social-emotional scores by engagement in special activities outside the home**

After accounting for socio-economic status

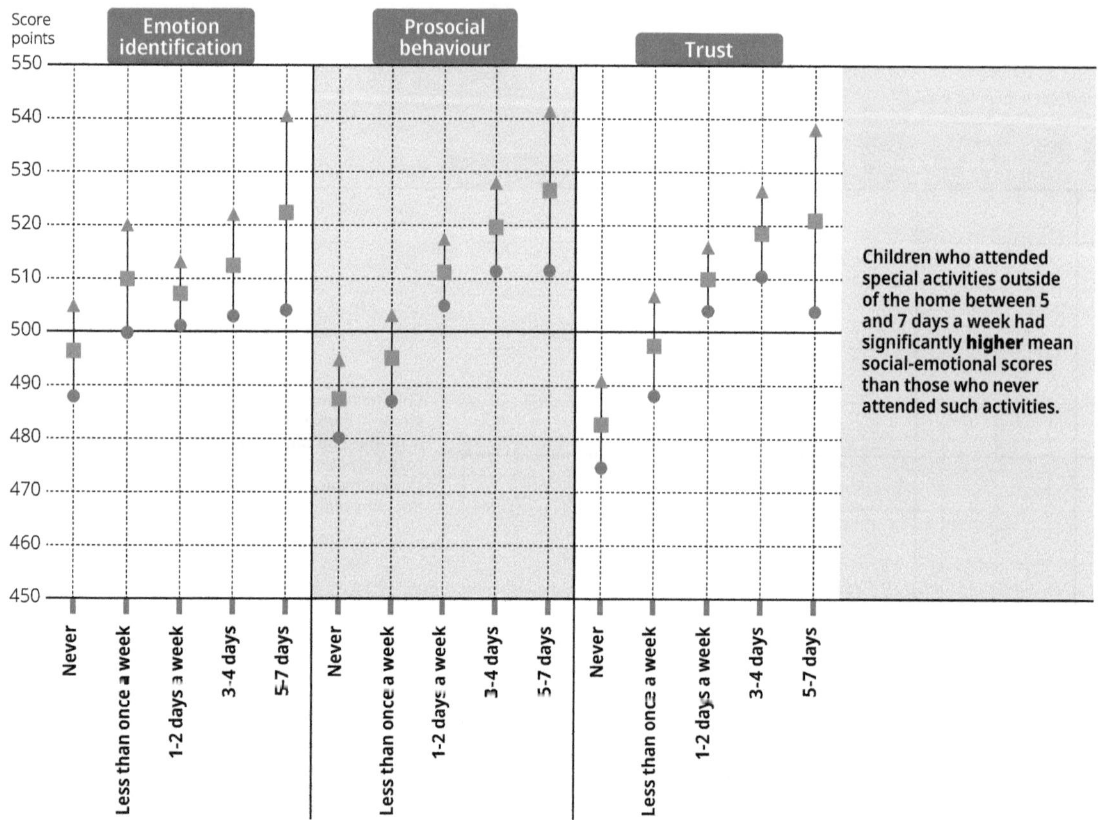

StatLink https://doi.org/10.1787/888934110638

ECEC attendance is not clearly related to children's social-emotional development

In England and Estonia, almost all children attend ECEC before the age of five, including those from disadvantaged backgrounds. In the United States, however, this is not the case. In 2017, 100% of three-year-olds in the United Kingdom participated in ECEC, compared to 91% in Estonia and 42% in the US, against an OECD average of 79% (OECD, 2019).

ECEC participation among children taking part in IELS in the United States varied significantly depending on their families' socio-economic status. Children from families in the top SES quartile were more likely (91%) to have attended ECEC than children from the bottom quartile (73%).

Unlike the associations with children's emergent literacy and numeracy, outlined in chapter 6, there were no clear relationships between whether children had participated in ECEC and their scores for social-emotional development. The study did, however, find that children who had started ECEC before three years of age were reported by teachers as having higher levels of trust than children who first attended at ages 3 or 4. At the same time, children who had started ECEC at three or four years of age were reported as being less disruptive than other children (Figure 4.17).

Children's social-emotional skills are associated with other areas of early learning

The relationships between children's social-emotional skills and other areas of early learning and development were significant (Figure 4.18). The social-emotional skills children develop in the first few years of their lives help them to regulate their emotions, connect well with others and operate in group settings, including playing with other children. This supports children's overall sense of well-being and happiness, and supports the ongoing development of other skills, such as oral language and self-regulation (Shuey and Kankaraš, 2018[1]).

Figure 4.16 **Social-emotional scores by mother's educational attainment**

Score-point differences between children whose mothers have at least a bachelor's degree and those whose mothers do not, before and after accounting for highest parental occupational status

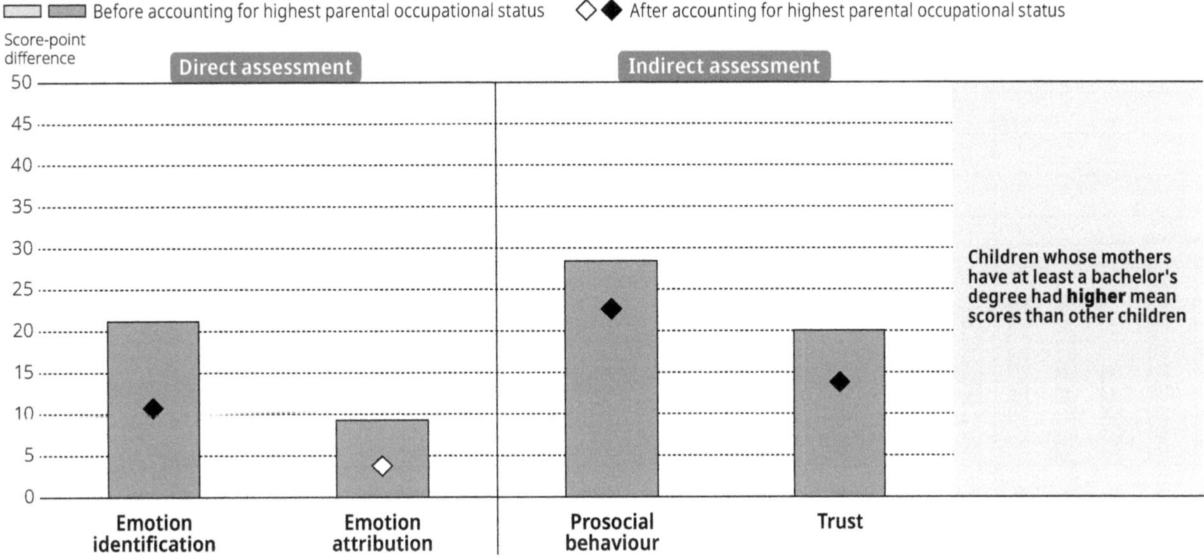

Note: Darker coloured markers indicate that the difference is statistically significant.

StatLink https://doi.org/10.1787/888934110657

Figure 4.17 **Trust and non-disruptive behaviour by age of starting ECEC**

Score-point differences between children who first attended ECEC when they were under 12 months and those who attended when they were two, three, and four years old, before and after accounting for socio-economic status.

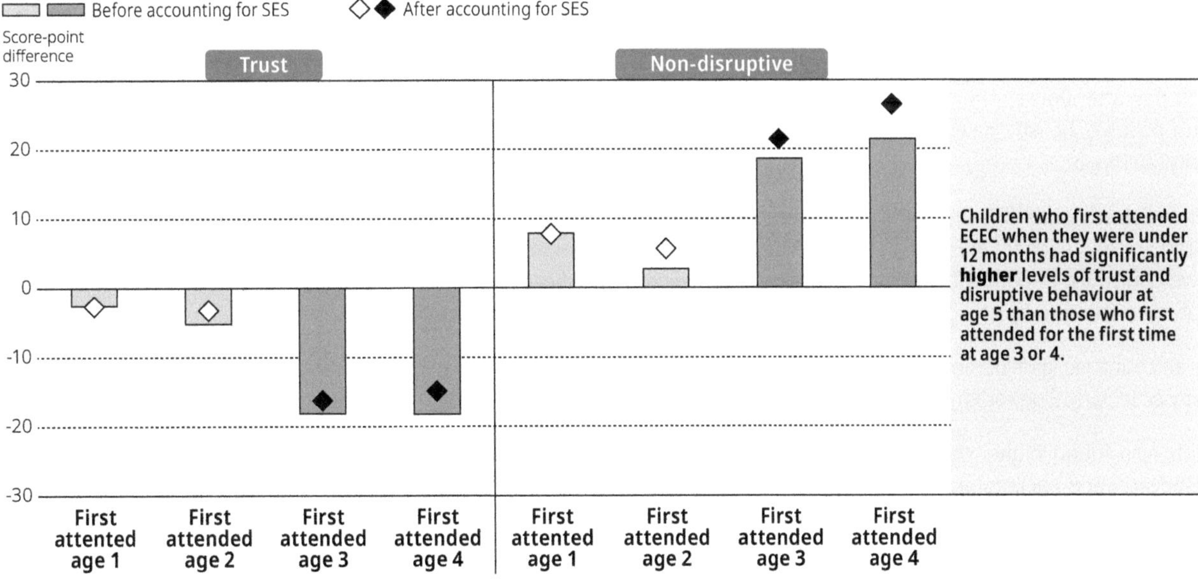

StatLink https://doi.org/10.1787/888934110676

After accounting for socio-economic status, children's social-emotional skills in England explained between 13% and 32% of the variation in emerging literacy, 5-27% in Estonia and 7-33% in the United States (Figure 4.18). These results demonstrate the significant relationship between social-emotional development and cognitive development.

Figure 4.18 Relationship between children's social-emotional skills and other early learning domains

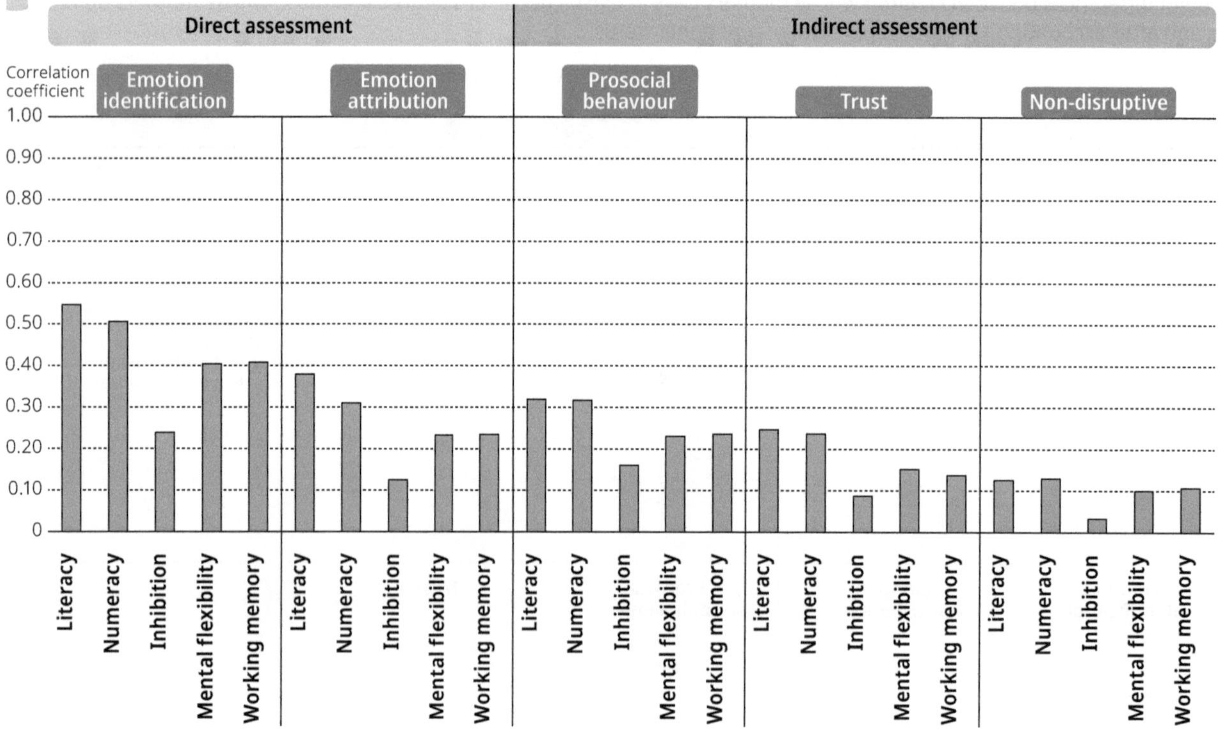

Note: All the correlations are statistically significant.
StatLink https://doi.org/10.1787/888934110695

CONCLUSIONS

Children's social-emotional skills are critical for well-being and happiness, and for their ongoing development and learning. The relationship between children's social-emotional skills and their development in other learning domains is significant. Thus, failing to pay attention to the development of children's social-emotional skills means foregoing a key means of supporting children's positive, holistic development and later success in school and beyond (Center on the Developing Child at Harvard University, 2016[20]).

Children in Estonia were able to identify others' emotions more accurately in the direct assessment than children in England and the United States. Teachers in Estonia also reported higher prosocial skills among the children in the study than teachers in the other two countries. In contrast, children in Estonia were considered more disruptive by their teachers than those in the other two countries. There were no significant differences in mean scores across the three countries for emotion attribution and trust.

In all three countries, girls demonstrated more developed social-emotional skills than boys across all five dimensions in the study. This was particularly true for emotion identification, prosocial behaviour and non-disruptive behaviour.

The study also found higher social-emotional scores amongst children from advantaged backgrounds compared to children from disadvantaged backgrounds. The largest difference associated with children's socio-economic background was in emotion identification and the least in non-disruptive behaviour.

Children with an immigrant background, or with a different home language from that used in the ECEC centre or school they attended, were reported by teachers as having lower levels of prosocial behaviours and trust than other children but also as less disruptive.

Having experienced learning or behavioural difficulties was negatively associated with children's social-emotional skills. Children with learning difficulties were found to have lower scores for empathy and lower ratings for prosocial behaviour and trust than other children. Children who had experienced social, emotional or behavioural difficulties had lower scores across the five social-emotional dimensions included in the study compared with children who had not experienced these difficulties.

Parental engagement with children, through a variety of activities, was positively related to children's social-emotional development. Children whose parents had back-and-forth conversations with them, such as on how the children feel, were more able to identify emotions in others. Other activities that parents engaged in that related positively to their children's social-emotional skills were reading to them from books and role-playing. Similarly, children whose parents who were involved in their ECEC centre or school or who took them to special activities also had higher social-emotional scores than other children.

References

Bowlby, J. (1969), *Attachment and Loss: Volume I, Attachment*, Basic Books, New York, https://www.abebe.org.br/files/John-Bowlby-Attachment-Second-Edition-Attachment-and-Loss-Series-Vol-1-1983.pdf (accessed on 31 July 2019). [18]

Buchanan, A., E. Flouri and **J. Brinke** (2002), "Emotional and behavioural problems in childhood and distress in adult life: Risk and protective factors", *Australian & New Zealand Journal of Psychiatry*, Vol. 36/4, pp. 521-527, https://doi.org/10.1046/j.1440-1614.2002.01048.x. [13]

Bush, G., P. Luu and **M. Posner** (2000), "Cognitive and emotional influences in anterior cingulate cortex", *Trends in Cognitive Sciences*, Vol. 4/6, pp. 215-222, https://doi.org/10.1016/s1364-6613(00)01483-2 (accessed on 30 July 2019). [2]

Caprara, G. et al. (2000), "Prosocial foundations of children's academic achievement", *Psychological Science*, Vol. 11/4, pp. 302-306, http://dx.doi.org/10.1111/1467-9280.00260 [10]

Center on the Developing Child at Harvard University (2016), *From Best Practices to Breakthrough Impacts: A Science-Based Approach to Building a More Promising Future for Young Children and Families*, Center on the Developing Child, https://developingchild.harvard.edu/resources/from-best-practices-to-breakthrough-impacts/ (accessed on 30 July 2019). [20]

Davidson, R. et al. (2002), "Neural and behavioral substrates of mood and mood regulation", *Biological Psychiatry*, Vol. 52/6, pp. 478-502, https://doi.org/10.1016/s0006-3223(02)01458-0 (accessed on 30 July 2019). [3]

Duncan, G. et al. (2007), "School readiness and later achievement", *Psychological Association*, Vol. 43/6, pp. 1428-1446, http://dx.doi.org/10.1037/[0012-1649.43.6.1428].supp. [8]

Flèche, S., W. Lekfuangfu and **A. Clark** (2019), "The long-lasting effects of family and childhood on adult wellbeing: Evidence from British cohort data", *Journal of Economic Behavior & Organization*, http://dx.doi.org/10.1016/J.JEBO.2018.09.018. [11]

Fontaine, N. et al. (2011), "Predictors and outcomes of joint trajectories of callous–unemotional traits and conduct problems in childhood", *Journal of Abnormal Psychology*, Vol. 120/3, pp. 730-742, http://dx.doi.org/10.1037/a0022620. [14]

Garber, J. and **K. Dodge** (1991), *The Development of Emotion Regulation and Dysregulation*, Cambridge University Press. [5]

Hogan, A., K. Scott and **C. Bauer** (1992), "The Adaptive Social Behavior Inventory (Asbi): A new assessment of social competence in high-risk three-year-olds", *Journal of Psychoeducational Assessment*, Vol. 10/3, pp. 230-239, http://dx.doi.org/10.1177/073428299201000303. [17]

Posner, M. and **M. Rothbart** (2000), "Developing mechanisms of self-regulation", *Development and Psychopathology*, Vol. 12/3, pp. 427-41, https://doi.org/10.1017/s0954579400003096 (accessed on 30 July 2019). [4]

Rutter, M., J. Kim-Cohen and **B. Maughan** (2006), "Continuities and discontinuities in psychopathology between childhood and adult life", *Journal of Child Psychology and Psychiatry*, Vol. 47/3-4, pp. 276-295, http://dx.doi.org/10.1111/j.1469-7610.2006.01614.x. [12]

Schoon, I. et al. (2015), "The impact of early life skills on later outcomes", *Report for the OECD*, No. EDU/EDPC(2015)26 JT03384682, http://discovery.ucl.ac.uk/10051902/1/Schoon_2015%20The%20Impact%20of%20Early%20Life%20Skills%20on%20Later%20Outcomes_%20Sept%20fin2015.pdf (accessed on 31 July 2019). [9]

Scientific Council on the Developing Child, N. (2004), "Children's emotional development is built into the architecture of their brains", *Working Paper*, No. 2, Center on the Developing Child, https://developingchild.harvard.edu/resources/childrens-emotional-development-is-built-into-the-architecture-of-their-brains/ (accessed on 30 July 2019). [6]

Shonkoff, J. and **D. Phillips** (2000), *From Neurons to Neighborhoods: The Science of Early Childhood Development*, National Acadamies Press, Washington, DC, https://www.nap.edu/catalog/9824/from-neurons-to-neighborhoods-the-science-of-early-childhood-development. [7]

Shuey, E. and **M. Kankaraš** (2018), "The power and promise of early learning", *OECD Education Working Papers*, No. 186, OECD Publishing, Paris, https://doi.org/10.1787/f9b2e53f-en. [33]

Sroufe, L. (2005), *The Development of the Person: The Minnesota Study of Risk and Adaptation from Birth to Adulthood*, Guilford Press. [19]

Strayer, J. (1993), "Children's concordant emotions and cognitions in response to observed emotions", *Child Development*, Vol. 64/1, pp. 188-201, http://dx.doi.org/10.1111/j.1467-8624.1993.tb02903.x. [15]

4

Notes

1. An immigrant background is defined as where both parents were born in a different country, or one parent, where information was only available for one parent.

2. The term social parent refers to an adult who is living in an information arrangement with a child's parent. Social siblings refer to the children of a child's social parent.

3. Lower than 5lbs 8oz or 2.5 kg

4. Tertiary education is defined as Level 5 and above on the International Standard Classification of Education (ISCED), i.e. generally at bachelor's degree level and above.

Children's skills in self-regulation

This chapter presents findings on the self-regulation of five-year-olds in England, Estonia and the United States. It describes how children's scores in inhibition, mental flexibility and working memory related to their individual and family characteristics, as well as their home learning environments. This is based on a direct assessment of children's skills and reports from the children's parents and teachers.

5

INTRODUCTION

The International Early Learning and Child Well-being Study (IELS) found variations in children's self-regulation skills across and within the countries taking part. Key differences in these skills were associated with children's socio-economic background, their home language, and their experiences of learning and social, emotional or behavioural difficulties.

Children in Estonia demonstrated high levels of skills across the three subdomains of self-regulation examined in IELS – inhibiting responses, mental flexibility and working memory. Children in England demonstrated similar skills to children in Estonia for mental flexibility and working memory, while children in the United States had similar inhibition skills to their Estonian peers.

Girls scored more highly on the three self-regulation subdomains when the results from the three countries were combined, but there were different gender patterns in each country. In Estonia, girls did better than boys across all three subdomains. In the United States girls were stronger than boys in inhibition and working memory, while in England, boys did better on inhibition. Otherwise, girls and boys had similar results.

Aspects of children's home environment were associated with their development of self-regulation skills, but to a lesser degree than for children's social-emotional skills, or emergent literacy or emergent numeracy skills. There were no clear relationships between children's participation in early childhood education and care (ECEC) and their self-regulation skills.

This chapter sets out:

- the critical importance of children's early skills in self-regulation for their well-being and later development
- the findings of the study in relation to the three aspects of self-regulation included in the study: inhibition, mental flexibility and working memory.

These findings are based on analysis of a representative sample of just under 7 000 five-year-olds in England, Estonia and the United States.

SELF-REGULATION SKILLS ARE CRITICAL FOR WELL-BEING AND EDUCATIONAL SUCCESS

The ability to regulate and manage thoughts, reactions and impulses is essential for ongoing learning, educational success, getting along well with others and maintaining good health (Diamond, 2013[1]; Eisenberg, Spinrad and Eggum, 2010[2]; McClelland et al., 2015[3]) . Self-regulation describes the capacity to use inhibition, mental flexibility and working memory – among other skills – to manage thoughts and actions (Zelazo, Blair and Willoughby, 2016[4]). These skills include the ability to direct and sustain short-term attention, inhibit impulse responses, revise initial plans, and retrieve information from memory (Shuey and Kankaraš, 2018[5]).

Early self-regulation skills are strong predictors of later health, education and socio-economic outcomes

The development of self-regulation skills in early childhood is associated with a wide range of positive outcomes. These include successful transition into school (Blair and Raver, 2015[5]; McClelland et al., 2007[6]; Morrison, Cameron and McClelland, 2010[7]), higher academic achievement in adolescence, better labour-market outcomes as adults, including employment levels and earnings, and better health outcomes (Duckworth, Quinn and Tsukayama, 2012[8]; Tangney, Baumeister and Boone, 2004[9]).

Self-regulation skills are important for children's transition to and participation in school (Blair and Peters Razza, 2007[10]; Neuenschwander et al., 2012[11]). The start of school can be a time of major change in the physical surroundings and people – including both other children and teachers – that children are accustomed to. It also presents a new set of learning expectations and routines to follow (Dockett and Perry, 2001[12]). Children must manage competing stimuli to navigate classroom activities. Self-regulation skills help children to learn new concepts and to engage successfully in classroom activities. These skills also enable children to interact productively with their teachers and peers while managing their own responses (Shonkoff and Phillips, 2000[13]). Such skills play an important role in academic achievement through late childhood and adolescence (Best, Miller and Naglieri, 2011[14]; Duncan et al., 2007[15]).

A child's ability to self-regulate is associated with the development of social-emotional, literacy and numeracy skills (Blair and Peters Razza, 2007[10]). For example, working memory (Raghubar, Barnes and Hecht, 2010[16]), inhibition and mental flexibility (Clark, Pritchard and Woodward, 2010[17]) are associated with the development of pre-arithmetic, simple and more complex mathematical skills.

Children with better-developed self-regulation skills in childhood also demonstrate better long-term health outcomes (Caspi et al., 1998[18]; Daly et al., 2015[19]; Moffitt et al., 2011[20]). These include lower rates of obesity in adolescence (Evans, Fuller-Rowell and Doan, 2012[21]) and lower levels of anxiety and depression (Blair and Peters Razza, 2007[10]; Buckner, Mezzacappa and Beardslee, 2009[22]). Children and adolescents with more developed self-regulation skills are also less likely to use drugs or receive a criminal conviction (Ayduk et al., 2000[23]; Caspi et al., 1998[18]; Duckworth, Tsukayama and May, 2010[24]; Moffitt et al., 2011[20]).

Children's environments influence the development of self-regulation skills

A combination of genetic and environmental factors shape the development of self-regulation skills (Bridgett et al., 2015[25]; McClelland et al., 2015[3]). Children exposed to poverty, low economic status, abuse or neglect in their home environment are more likely to display deficits in their self-regulation skills when compared to children living in more enabling environments (Noble, Norman and Farah, 2005[26]; Raver, Blair and Willoughby, 2013[27]).

Adverse childhood experiences and toxic stress can significantly impair the early self-regulation development of children. Exposure to adverse home environments can limit their opportunities to develop their self-regulation skills. Negative early experiences, including multiple and chronic environmental stressors, can cause structural changes in the neural connections of the areas of the brain that control self-regulation (Nelson et al., 2007[28]; McEwen, Nasca and Gray, 2016[29]). Children exposed to cumulative risks are also more likely to have parents who do not provide opportunities for a child to practise their self-regulation skills (Wachs, Gurkas and Kontos, 2004[30]; Fuller et al., 2010[31]).

Disparities in socio-economic background are associated with differences in the physical structure and functioning of the parts of the brain that control self-regulation (Hackman and Farah, 2009[32]). The functioning of the prefrontal cortex in children from low socio-economic backgrounds who are exposed to chronic environmental stressors, for example, is similar to that of individuals with damage to the prefrontal cortex (Kishiyama et al., 2009[33]).

A positive home environment and high-quality early childhood education and care experiences support the development of self-regulation skills

Self-regulation skills are malleable (Raver and Blair, 2016[37]). Emotionally positive parent-child relationships contribute to self-regulation skills across the early years. Parenting styles that include clear and consistent rules and expectations encourage the positive development of self-regulation skills (Blair and Raver, 2012[36]). For example, parenting styles that focus on children's autonomy within set limits predict stronger self-regulation development in children than parenting styles focused on compliance (Bernier, Carlson and Whipple, 2010[37]).

Organised and predictable home environments provide children with a context where they can develop their self-regulation skills (McClelland et al., 2018[38]). Interactions between children and their parents and caregivers help children to understand their emotions and to regulate their behaviour. This, in turn, allows children to regulate their responses to distracting stimuli in their environment (Heatherton and Wagner, 2011[39]).

As with the home environment, structured and predictable environments in ECEC are important for children's self-regulation, engagement and academic outcomes (Ponitz et al., 2009[40]). High-quality ECEC environments support the development of children's early self-regulation skills.

This study focuses on the key self-regulation skills of inhibition, mental flexibility and working memory

Self-regulation skills are highly inter-related (Anderson and Reidy, 2012[41]). Completing everyday tasks requires adequate development in all of the inter-dependent parts.

A large body of literature has emphasised a number of key self-regulation skills (Diamond and Lee, 2011[42]; Garon, Bryson and Smith, 2008[43]). These have mostly centred on the influence of inhibition, mental flexibility and working memory skills on later outcomes. These three skills together are often referred to as executive function. Executive function skills make up the cognitive component of self-regulation. IELS operationalised self-regulation in the direct assessment as: 1) inhibition - the ability to control impulses and reactions; 2) mental flexibility - the ability to shift between rules according to changing circumstances; and 3) working memory - the ability to retain and process information (Figure 5.1).

Figure 5.1 **The three components of self-regulation in IELS**

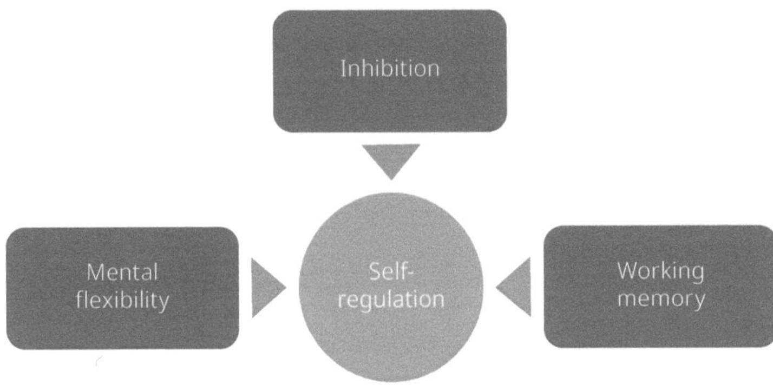

Each of the skills that makes up self-regulation in IELS were directly measured using a set of specific tasks delivered on a tablet and involved children engaging with game-like activities. Audio and engaging illustrations guided the children through the activities (see Figure 5.2 for example).

Information on children's self-regulation development was also collected through questionnaires administered to children's parents and teachers. Parents and teachers were asked to assess each child's overall self-regulation development, defined as whether children were attentive, organised or in control of their actions.

Figure 5.2 **Children were asked to remember and recall where the zebra was sitting on the bus**

OVERALL FINDINGS

Estonian children have high overall levels of self-regulation skills

The study found significant differences across England, Estonia and the United States in children's self-regulation skills. Children in Estonia scored highly across all three subdomains in the direct assessment of self-regulation. Children in England demonstrated similar levels of skills to Estonian children in mental flexibility and working memory, while children from the United States had similar inhibition scores to Estonian children. The mean scores for each country are set out in Table 5.1.

Table 5.1 **Mean self-regulation scores of countries that participated in IELS**

	Inhibition	Mental flexibility	Working memory
Estonia	520	511	521
England	460	513	516
United States	521	477	464

StatLink https://doi.org/10.1787/888934110714

Figure 5.3 shows the distribution of scores for inhibition, mental flexibility and working memory by each country. Children in Estonia and the United States demonstrated similar levels of skill in inhibiting responses, whereas a greater proportion of children in England scored below the overall mean. The findings on mental flexibility in England and Estonia were very similar, with almost identical percentages of children at the highest levels of this skill. The United States had a significantly lower overall mean than the other two countries, partly due to having a lower proportion of children at the upper skill levels. The results for working memory are similar to those of mental flexibility. Once again, the findings from England and Estonia were closely matched, with comparable proportions of children at the highest and lowest ends of the skill distribution. The United States had a lower overall mean and a smaller percentage of children with the highest skill level in working memory.

Figure 5.3 **Distribution of self-regulation scores, by country**

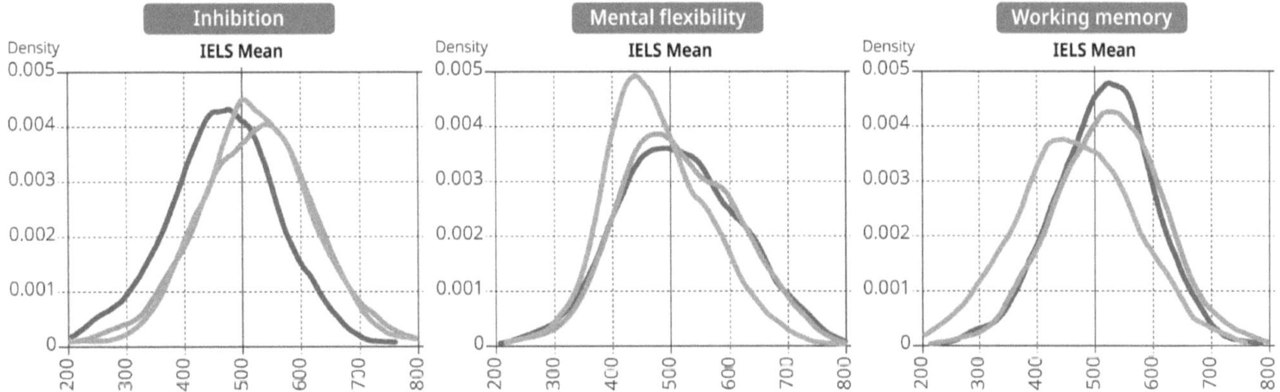

Older children have higher self-regulation scores

As in other areas of the study, the self-regulation scores of older children were higher than younger children between the ages of five and six, as shown in Figure 5.4. The score point difference between children who were five years, one month and children who were six years were 81 points, 50 points and 67 points for inhibition, mental flexibility and working memory respectively. The average difference in the inhibition and mental flexibility outcomes of children between the ages of five years one month and six years were similar across the three countries participating in IELS. The average difference in working memory outcomes between those age groups was similar in both England and the United States, but smaller in Estonia.

Figure 5.4 **Inhibition, mental flexibility and working memory scores by age in months, by country**

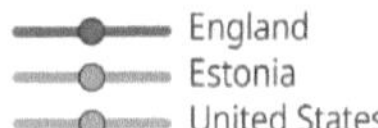

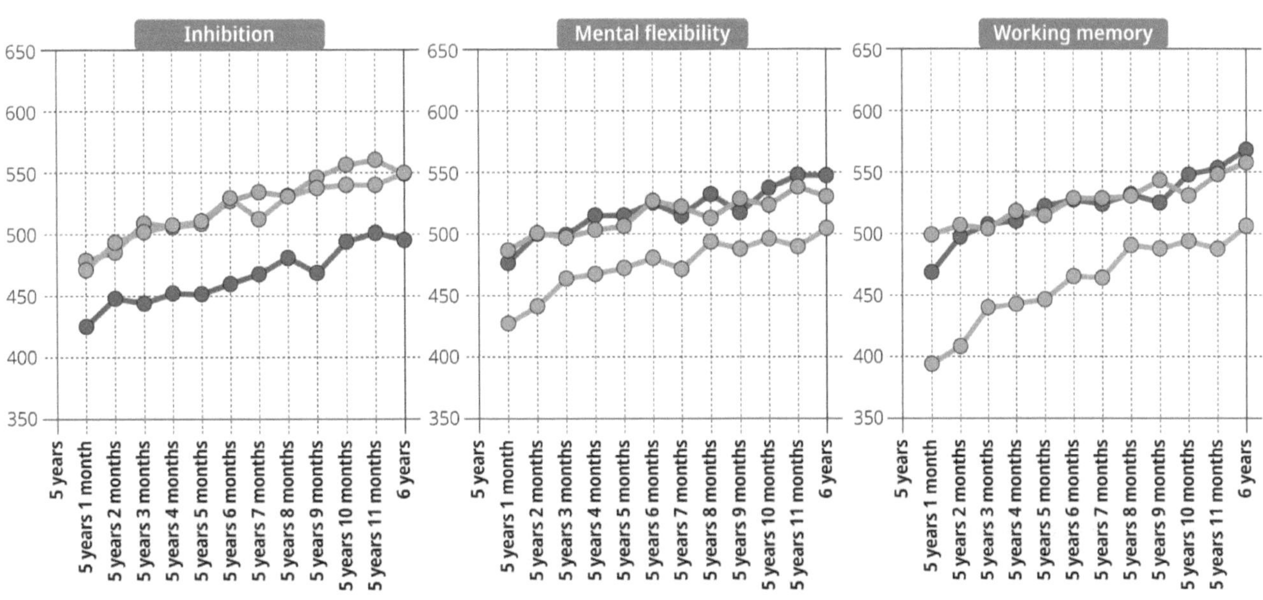

StatLink https://doi.org/10.1787/888934110733

Clear gender differences are only apparent in Estonia

There was no consistent or significant gender pattern in the findings across the three countries. When the results from each country are combined, however, girls scored more highly than boys in inhibition, mental flexibility and working memory. Estonia had the most pronounced gender gap in favour of girls, with a significantly higher mean than for boys in each self-regulation subdomain. In England, boys did slightly better than girls in inhibition, but there were no gender differences in mental flexibility or working memory. In the United States, girls had significantly stronger inhibition and working memory skills than boys, but similar mental flexibility skills. Figure 5.5 shows the aggregate findings by gender across all three countries.

Figure 5.5 **Mean self-regulation scores of children, by gender**

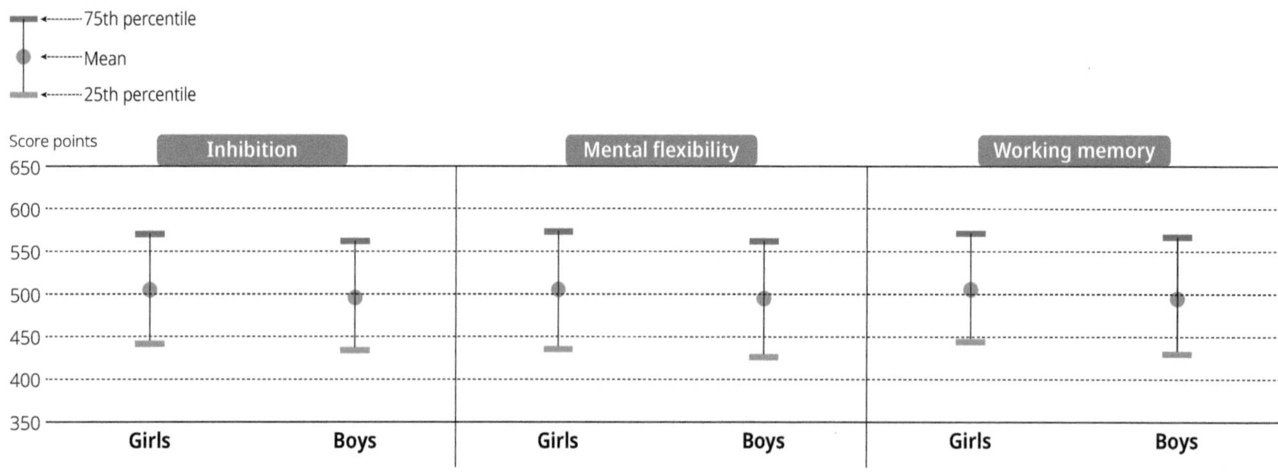

Note: Differences are statistically significant, except for mental flexibility and working memory scores at the 75th percentile.

StatLink https://doi.org/10.1787/888934110752

Parents and teachers reported that girls had stronger self-regulation skills than boys. The size of these gender differences were similar across England, Estonia and the United States. Similar to other findings in this study, parents had a more positive view of their children's skill levels than teachers, as illustrated in Figure 5.6.

Figure 5.6 **Children's self-regulation development by gender, as reported by their parents and teachers**

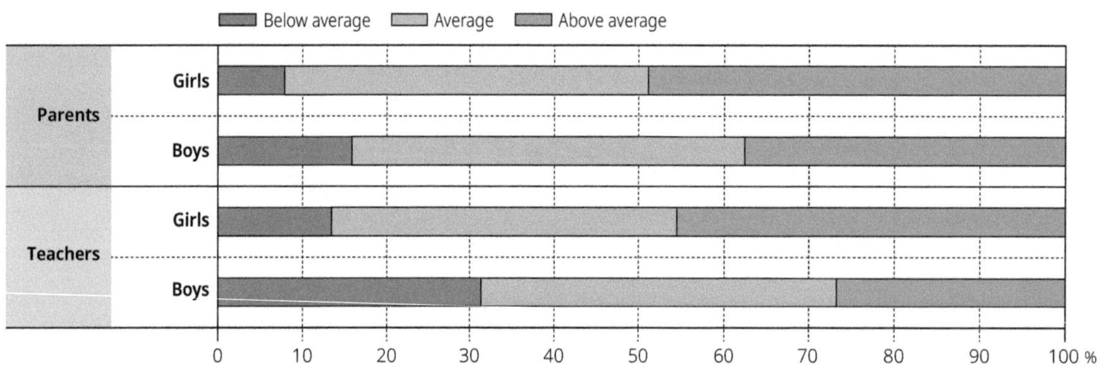

StatLink https://doi.org/10.1787/888934110771

Children from more advantaged backgrounds have stronger self-regulation than other children

Many studies have found that the socio-economic status (SES) of children's families is associated with their learning outcomes. Nonetheless, the extent to which a child's background is related to their education outcomes varies widely across countries. Some education systems are largely successful in mitigating children's disadvantaged backgrounds whereas other education systems struggle to do so effectively.

In IELS, a child's socio-economic status was related to their self-regulation scores across all three countries, particularly for mental flexibility and working memory (Figure 5.7).

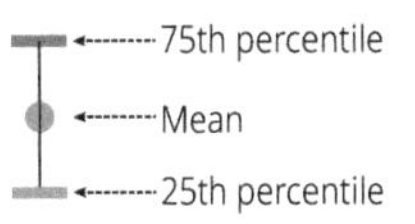

Figure 5.7 **Self-regulation scores of children by socio-economic status**

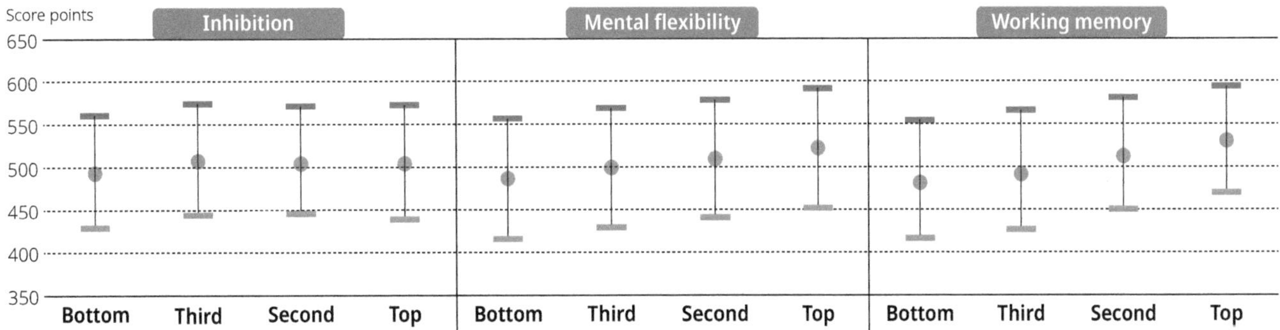

Note: Differences in mean scores between top and bottom quartiles significant for all self-regulation scores. Differences at the 25th and 75th percentile between top and bottom quartiles significant for mental flexibility and working memory, but not for inhibition.

StatLink https://doi.org/10.1787/888934110790

There were no significant differences in children's inhibition scores between the top and bottom socio-economic quartiles in either England or Estonia, whereas such differences were evident in the United States. In England and the United States, children from high socio-economic backgrounds demonstrated significantly higher scores in mental flexibility than children from low socio-economic backgrounds. Children from high socio-economic backgrounds had higher working memory scores in all three countries.

Parents and teachers were more likely to report children from higher socio-economic groups as having greater self-regulation skills than children from lower socio-economic groups (Figure 5.8), consistent with the findings from the direct assessment. As noted above, parents were more positive about their children's level of skills than teachers.

Figure 5.8 **Parent and teacher reports on children's self-regulation development, by socioeconomic status**

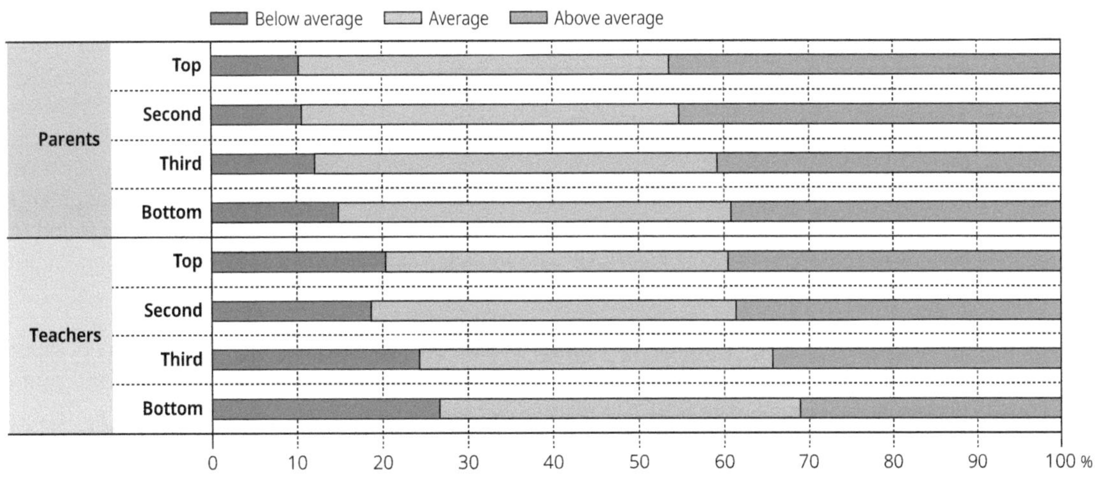

StatLink https://doi.org/10.1787/888934110809

Having an immigrant background is not related to children's self-regulation skills

The study found no significant differences in self-regulation scores for children from families with an immigrant background once socio-economic status and home language were taken into account. Children with two parents born in a country other than that in which the child participated in IELS (or the sole parent if there was only information about one) were considered to have an immigrant background. Approximately 12% of children across the three countries came from an immigrant background.

There were no significant differences between the perceptions of immigrant and non-immigrant parents of their children's self-regulation skills or of teachers' ratings of children from immigrant and non-immigrant children. There were also no significant differences in the ratings by parents and teachers of girls and boys with immigrant backgrounds, and nor were there significant differences across countries.

Children's home language is negatively associated with children's self-regulation

Parents of children in the study were also asked to identify whether one or both parents primarily spoke a different language at home than the language of the ECEC centre or school that the child attended.[1] Across the three countries, 13% of the children in this study had a different home language. In the United States, 20% of children had a different home language, compared to 16% in England and 6% in Estonia.

The direct assessments were carried out in English in England and the United States, and in Estonian or Russian in Estonia. The aggregate results for all three countries show that children with a home language different from the language of assessment had lower scores in inhibition, mental flexibility and working memory than other children, after accounting for socio-economic status. These findings are shown in Figure 5.9.

Figure 5.9 **Difference in self-regulation scores by home language**

Score point difference in self-regulation outcomes between children of parents (or single parent) who both speak the assessment language and those of parents where at least one parent primarily speaks another language, before and after accounting for socioeconomic status

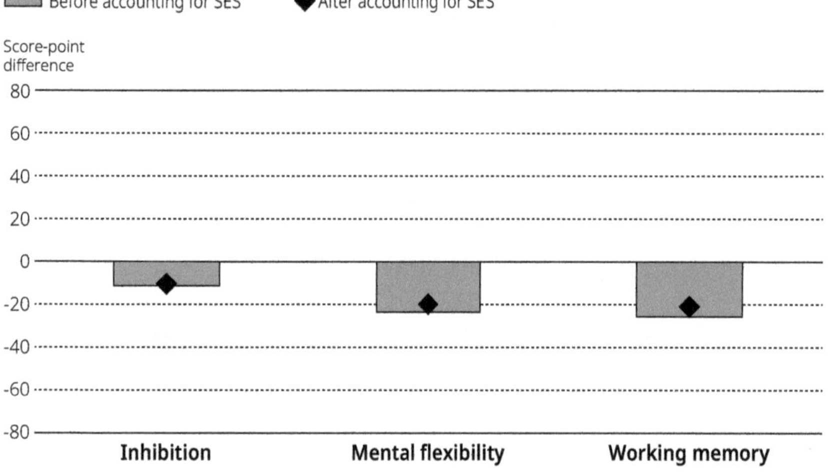

StatLink https://doi.org/10.1787/888934110828

In Estonia, children with a home language different from the language of assessment had lower scores in inhibition, mental flexibility and working memory than other children. In the United States, significant effects for home language were found for mental flexibility. In England, there were no differences in the levels of self-regulation skills between children with a non-English home language and other children.

When asked to report on their perceptions of children's overall self-regulation development, parents and teachers did not report significant differences in the self-regulation skills of children who have a home language that is different from their ECEC centre or school compared to other children, as set out in Figure 5.10.

Learning and behavioural difficulties are associated with poorer self-regulation

Parents also provided information on whether their child was premature or had a low birthweight,[2] learning difficulties (e.g. speech or language delay, intellectual disability), or social, emotional or behavioural difficulties. Across the three countries, the mean percentage of children with at least one of these challenges was 24%, with a mean of 9% having experienced low birthweight or premature birth, 11% having experienced learning difficulties and 10% having experienced social, emotional or behavioural difficulties. On average across countries, 5% of children had experienced two of these challenges and 1%, on average, experienced all three.

Overall, parents in England and Estonia reported slightly fewer children with these challenges than parents in the United States. Estonian parents reported the smallest proportion of children who experienced low birthweight or premature birth while parents in England reported the smallest proportion of children with social, emotional or behavioural difficulties.

Figure 5.10 **Parent and teacher reports on children's self-regulation development, by home language**

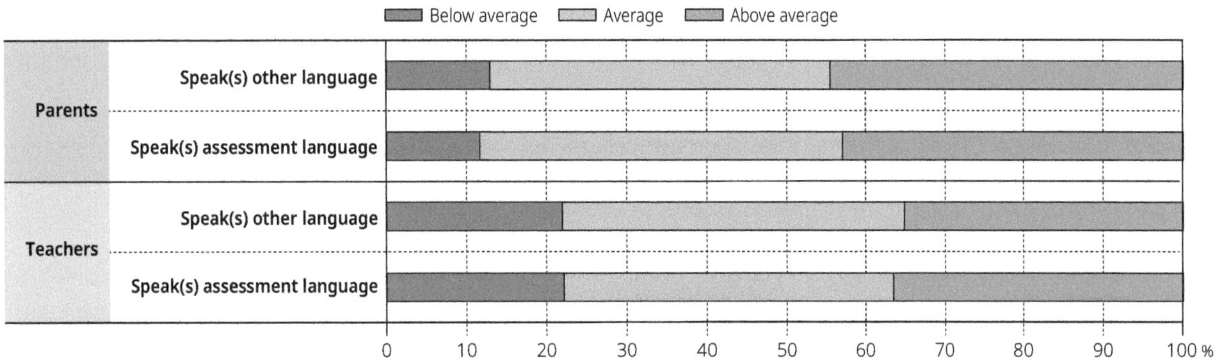

StatLink ⬛ https://doi.org/10.1787/888934110847

There were no significant gender differences in the proportion of children who had a low birthweight or were premature. Boys were twice as likely as girls to be reported by their parents as having learning difficulties or social, emotional or behavioural difficulties.

Having learning difficulties was associated with lower scores in all three countries for mental flexibility and working memory. In England, there were no differences in the inhibition outcomes of children who had experienced learning difficulties and those who had not after accounting for socio-economic status and the experience of other early difficulties. Having experienced learning difficulties was related to all self-regulation outcomes in Estonia and the United States. Having experienced social, emotional or behavioural difficulties was associated with lower scores in England and Estonia on mental flexibility and working memory, and on working memory in the United States. The aggregate effects are illustrated in Figure 5.11.

Figure 5.11 **Differences in self-regulation by experience of early difficulties**

Score-point differences between children who had and had not experienced early difficulties, before and after accounting for socio-economic status

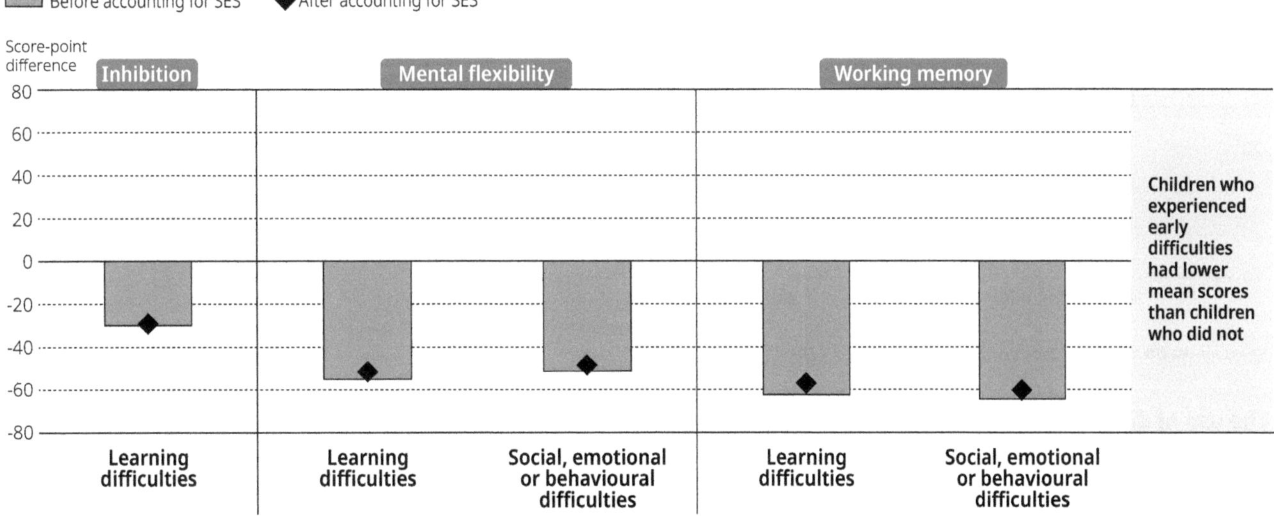

Note: Statistically significant differences are shown in a darker tone.
StatLink ⬛ https://doi.org/10.1787/888934110866

Access to children's books is linked to better working memory

Children's home environments are critical for their early learning and development. Parents were asked how often they undertook certain activities with their children, as well as other aspects of the home environment such as the presence of children's books.

Parents' activities with their children do not show the same strength of association with children's self-regulation skills as they do with other areas of children's development in this study. In addition, some parental activities appear to be more highly correlated with children's self-regulation skills in one country but not in the others. For example, reading to children from books was positively associated with children's working memory scores in Estonia but not in England or the United States. Having children's books in the home was positively associated with children's working memory skills in all three countries and with children's mental flexibility in England and Estonia. There was no relationship between the number of children's books in the home and their inhibition scores at an aggregate level.

Taking children to a special or paid activity such as sports or cultural activities was associated with higher levels of working memory in England and Estonia, but not in the United States. The frequency with which a child is taken to a special or paid activity outside of the home was also related to their inhibition scores in Estonia and their mental flexibility scores in England.

Mothers' education levels correlate positively with their children's self-regulation

Parents with higher levels of education are more likely to engage their children in activities that help children to learn, such as reading to them from books and being involved in their children's ECEC centre or school (Sylva et al., 2003[46]). In addition, studies on children's early development have found independent positive effects of mothers' education in particular on children's learning. As noted in Chapter 3, the mothers of the children sampled in Estonia were much more likely to have a bachelor's degree (53%) than those in either England (40%) or the United States (39%).

In comparing children whose mothers had at least a bachelor's degree with other children, higher mental flexibility scores were found in England and the United States and higher scores for working memory in England and Estonia. At the aggregate level, the findings for mental flexibility and working memory were both significant (Figure 5.12). There was no relationship between mothers' educational qualifications and inhibition.

Figure 5.12 **Differences in self-regulation scores by mother's education**

Score point difference in self-regulation outcomes between children of mothers who had completed a Bachelor's degree and those who had not, before and after accounting for socioeconomic status

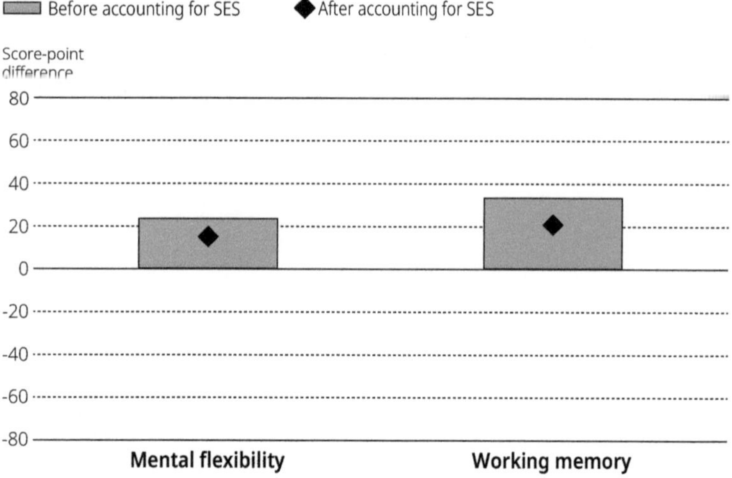

StatLink https://doi.org/10.1787/888934110885

The use of digital devices has no clear relationship with self-regulation skills

On average, 83% of children across the three participating countries used a digital device at least once a week, with 42%, on average, using them every day. Only 7% of the children across countries never or hardly ever used a device, with an average of 10% of children using digital devices at least monthly, but not weekly.

There was no clear relationship between the frequency of device use and children's self-regulation skills. Children in Estonia and the United States who regularly used a device had higher mental flexibility scores than children who did not use a device regularly, although there were no such differences amongst children in England. There were also some positive associations for working memory in England and for inhibition in Estonia, but these associations were not apparent in the other two countries.

There are few associations between household composition and children's self-regulation skills

On average across the three participating countries, 86% of children in IELS lived in two-parent households. At an aggregate level, there were no differences in the inhibition and working memory scores of children from one- and two-parent households, after accounting for socio-economic status. Children in England, however, who lived in single-parent households had lower mental flexibility scores than other children. In Estonia, children who lived in single-parent households had higher scores for working memory than other children.

The number of siblings a child had also showed little relationship with their self-regulation skills, although children with one sibling had better scores for working memory than children with no siblings.

The effects of early childhood education and care are equivocal

In England and Estonia, almost all children in the study had attended ECEC, including children from disadvantaged backgrounds. In the United States, however, this was not the case.

In the United States, ECEC participation varied significantly depending on the socio-economic status of the child's family. Children from advantaged families were more likely (91%) to have attended ECEC than children from disadvantaged families (73%). Rates of ECEC attendance did not vary significantly on the basis of ethnicity or race.

Unlike the relationship between ECEC and children's literacy and numeracy skills, as outlined in Chapter 6, the study did not find significant or consistent findings in relation to children's attendance of ECEC and their self-regulation skills. This was regardless of the age children started ECEC or the intensity of ECEC participation, i.e. whether they attended part time or full time.

Self-regulation skills correlate more strongly with cognitive skills than social-emotional skills

Self-regulation skills correlate more closely with children's emergent literacy and numeracy scores than to their social-emotional learning. These associations are stronger for mental flexibility and working memory than for inhibition, as illustrated in Figure 5.13. Mental flexibility and working memory had stronger relationships with the other early learning dimensions in the study than inhibition.

Figure 5.13 **Correlations between children's self-regulation and other early learning scores**

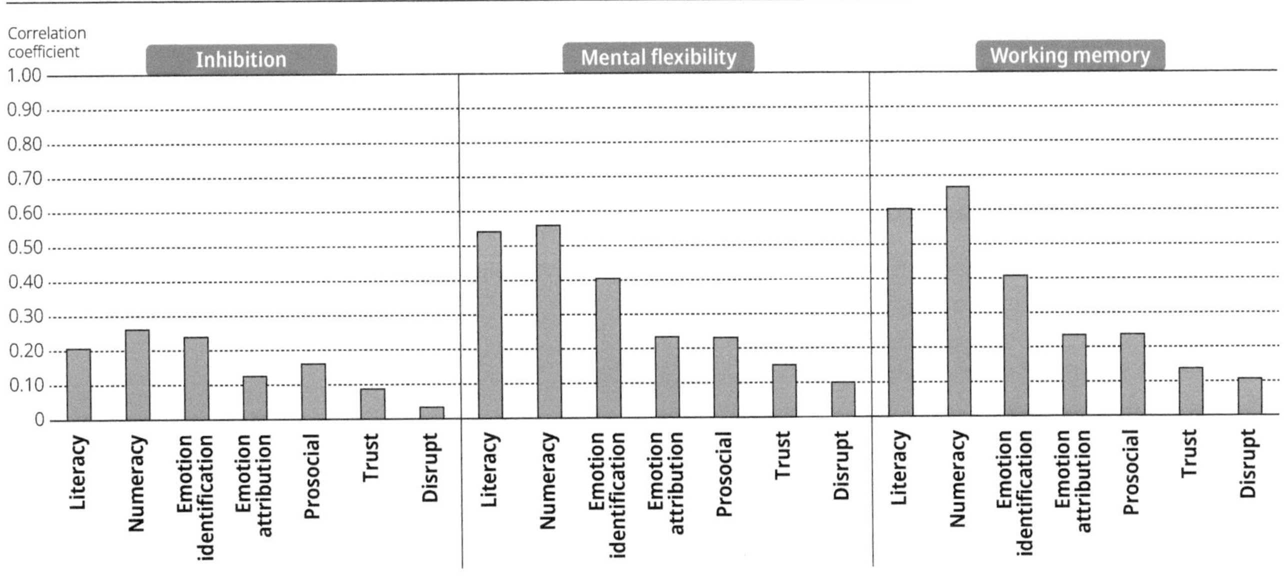

StatLink https://doi.org/10.1787/888934110904

CONCLUSIONS

Children in Estonia demonstrated relatively high levels of self-regulation skills across the three elements of self-regulation directly measured in this study: inhibition, mental flexibility and working memory. Children in England had similar levels of skills to Estonian children in mental flexibility and working memory, but less so for inhibition. Children in the United States demonstrated inhibition skills at a similar level to those of Estonian children, but had lower scores for mental flexibility and working memory.

The study did not find clear or consistent gender differences in children's self-regulation skills in the direct assessment, although there were differences at an individual country level. In Estonia, girls had higher self-regulation skills than boys across inhibition, mental flexibility and working memory. Girls in the United States did somewhat better than boys in inhibition and working memory, whereas in England boys had stronger skills than girls in inhibition. The reports from parents and teachers in all three countries, however, consistently rated girls' skills in self-regulation as higher than those of boys.

The background factors that were most closely associated with children's self-regulation levels were their socio-economic background, home language and the prevalence of learning difficulties or social, emotional or behavioural difficulties. The self-regulation sub-domains most highly correlated to these factors were mental flexibility and working memory.

Having children's books in the home was positively associated with children's working memory scores in each country, and with children's mental flexibility in England and Estonia.

Children's self-regulation skills relate to their ability to concentrate, learn and retain information. For this reason, it is unsurprising that the study found clear associations between children's self-regulation skills, particularly for mental flexibility and working memory, and their development in emergent literacy and emergent numeracy. The study also found positive relationships between children's self-regulation skills and their social-emotional skills, although to a lesser extent than with cognitive skills.

References

Anderson, P. and **N. Reidy** (2012), "Assessing executive function in preschoolers", *Neuropsychological Review*, Vol. 22/4, pp. 345-360, https://doi.org/10.1007/s11065-012-9220-3. [43]

Ayduk, O. et al. (2000), "Regulating the interpersonal self: Strategic self-regulation for coping with rejection sensitivity", *Journal of Personality and Social Psychology*, Vol. 79/5, pp. 776-792, https://psycnet.apa.org/doi/10.1037/0022-3514.79.5.776 (accessed on 28 June 2019). [24]

Bernier, A., S. Carlson and **N. Whipple** (2010), "From external regulation to self-regulation: Early parenting precursors of young children's executive functioning", *Child Development*, Vol. 81/1, pp. 326-339, http://dx.doi.org/10.1111/j.1467-8624.2009.01397.x. [39]

Best, J., P. Miller and **J. Naglieri** (2011), "Relations between executive function and academic achievement from ages 5 to 17 in a large, representative national sample", *Learning and Individual Differences*, Vol. 21/4, pp. 327-336, http://dx.doi.org/10.1016/J.LINDIF.2011.01.007. [15]

Blair, C. and **R. Peters Razza** (2007), "Relating effortful control, executive function, and false belief understanding to emerging math and literacy ability in kindergarten", *Child Development*, Vol. 78/2, pp. 647-663, https://onlinelibrary.wiley.com/doi/pdf/10.1111/j.1467-8624.2007.01019.x (accessed on 28 June 2019). [11]

Blair, C. and **C. Raver** (2015), "School readiness and self-regulation. A developmental psychobiological approach", *Annual Review of Psychology*, Vol. 66/1, pp. 711-731, http://dx.doi.org/10.1146/annurev-psych-010814-015221. [6]

Blair, C. and **C. Raver** (2012), "Individual development and evolution: Experiential canalization of self-regulation", *Developmental Psychology*, Vol. 48/3, pp. 647-657, http://dx.doi.org/10.1037/a0026472. [38]

Booth, A., E. Hennessy and **O. Doyle** (2018), "Self-regulation: Learning across disciplines", *Journal of Child and Family Studies*, Vol. 27/12, pp. 3767–3781, https://doi.org/10.1007/s10826-018-1202-5. [47]

Bridgett, D. et al. (2015), "Intergenerational transmission of self-regulation: A multidisciplinary review and integrative conceptual framework", *Psychological Bulletin*, Vol. 141/3, pp. 602-654, http://dx.doi.org/10.1037/a0038662. [26]

Buckner, J., E. Mezzacappa and **W. Beardslee** (2009), "Self-regulation and Its relations to adaptive functioning in low income youths", *American Journal of Orthopsychiatry*, Vol. 79/1, pp. 19-30, http://dx.doi.org/10.1037/a0014796. [23]

Caspi, A. et al. (1998), "Early failure in the labor market: Childhood and adolescent predictors of unemployment in the transition to adulthood", *American Sociological Review*, Vol. 63/3, pp. 424-451, http://dx.doi.org/10.2307/2657557 (accessed on 28 June 2019). [19]

Clark, C., V. Pritchard and **L. Woodward** (2010), "Preschool executive functioning abilities predict early mathematics achievement", *Developmental Psychology*, Vol. 46/5, pp. 1176-1191, http://dx.doi.org/10.1037/a0019672. [18]

Daly, M. et al. (2015), "Childhood self-control and unemployment throughout the life span: Evidence from two British cohort studies", *Psychological Science*, Vol. 26/6, pp. 709-723, http://dx.doi.org/10.1177/0956797615569001. [20]

Diamond, A. (2013), "Executive functions", *Annual Review of Psychology*, Vol. 64/1, pp. 135-168, http://dx.doi.org/10.1146/annurev-psych-113011-143750. [1]

Diamond, A. and **K. Lee** (2011), "Interventions shown to aid executive function development in children 4 to 12 years old", *Science*, Vol. 333/6045, pp. 959-964, http://dx.doi.org/10.1126/science.1204529. [44]

Dockett, S. and **B. Perry** (2001), "Starting school: Effective transitions", *Early Childhood Research & Practice*, Vol. 3/2, https://eric.ed.gov/?id=ED458041 (accessed on 3 July 2019). [13]

Duckworth, A., P. Quinn and **E. Tsukayama** (2012), "What No Child Left Behind leaves behind: The roles of IQ and self-control in predicting standardized achievement test scores and report card grades", *Journal of Educational Psychology*, Vol. 104/2, pp. 439-451, http://dx.doi.org/10.1037/a0026280. [9]

Duckworth, A., E. Tsukayama and **H. May** (2010), "Establishing causality using longitudinal hierarchical linear modeling: An illustration predicting achievement from self-control", *Social Psychological and Personality Science*, Vol. 1/4, pp. 311-317, http://dx.doi.org/10.1177/1948550609359707. [25]

Duncan, G. et al. (2007), "School readiness and later achievement", *Developmental Psychology*, Vol. 43/6, pp. 1428-1446, http://dx.doi.org/10.1037/[0012-1649.43.6.1428].supp. [16]

Eisenberg, N., T. Spinrad and **N. Eggum** (2010), "Emotion-related self-regulation and its relation to children's maladjustment", *Annual Review of Clinical Psychology*, Vol. 6, pp. 495-525, http://dx.doi.org/10.1146/annurev.clinpsy.121208.131208. [2]

Evans, G., T. Fuller-Rowell and **S. Doan** (2012), "Childhood cumulative risk and obesity: The mediating role of self-regulatory ability", *Pediatrics*, Vol. 129/1, pp. e68-e73, http://dx.doi.org/10.1542/peds.2010-3647. [22]

Fuller, B. et al. (2010), "Maternal practices that influence Hispanic infants' health and cognitive growth", *Pediatrics*, Vol. 125/2, pp. e324-e332, http://dx.doi.org/10.1542/peds.2009-0496. [32]

Garon, N., S. Bryson and **I. Smith** (2008), "Executive function in preschoolers: A review using an integrative framework", *Psychological Bulletin*, Vol. 134/1, pp. 31-60, http://dx.doi.org/10.1037/0033-2909.134.1.31. [45]

Hackman, D. and **M. Farah** (2009), "Socioeconomic status and the developing brain", *Trends in Cognitive Sciences*, Vol. 13/2, pp. 65-73, http://dx.doi.org/10.1016/J.TICS.2008.11.003. [33]

Heatherton, T. and **D. Wagner** (2011), "Cognitive neuroscience of self-regulation failure", *Trends in Cognitive Sciences*, Vol. 15/3, pp. 132-139, http://dx.doi.org/10.1016/J.TICS.2010.12.005. [41]

Kishiyama, M. et al. (2009), "Socioeconomic disparities affect prefrontal function in children", *Journal of Cognitive Neuroscience*, Vol. 21/6, pp. 1106-1115, http://dx.doi.org/10.1162/jocn.2009.21101. [34]

McClelland, M. et al. (2007), "Links between behavioral regulation and preschoolers' literacy, vocabulary, and math skills", *Developmental Psychology*, Vol. 43/4, pp. 947–959, http://dx.doi.org/10.1037/0012-1649.43.4.947. [7]

McClelland, M. et al. (2018), "Self-regulation", in *Handbook of Life Course Health Development*, Springer International Publishing, Cham, http://dx.doi.org/10.1007/978-3-319-47143-3_12. [40]

McClelland, M. et al. (2015), "Development and self-regulation", in *Handbook of Child Psychology and Developmental Science*, John Wiley & Sons, Inc., http://dx.doi.org/10.1002/9781118963418.childpsy114. [3]

McClelland, M. et al. (2010), "Self-regulation: Integration of cognition and emotion", in *The Handbook of Life-Span Development*, John Wiley & Sons, Inc., http://dx.doi.org/10.1002/9780470880166.hlsd001015. [48]

McEwen, B., C. Nasca and **J. Gray** (2016), "Stress effects on neuronal structure: Hippocampus, amygdala, and prefrontal cortex", *Neuropsychopharmacology*, Vol. 41/1, pp. 3-23, http://dx.doi.org/10.1038/npp.2015.171. [30]

Moffitt, T. et al. (2011), "A gradient of childhood self-control predicts health, wealth, and public safety", *Proceedings of the National Academy of Sciences of the United States of America*, Vol. 108/7, pp. 2693-2698, http://dx.doi.org/10.1073/pnas.1010076108. [21]

Morrison, F., C. Cameron and **M. McClelland** (2010), "Self-regulation and academic achievement in the transition to school", in Calkins, S. and M. Bell (eds.), *Human Brain Development: Child Development at the Intersection of Emotion and Cognition*, American Psychological Association, Washington, DC, http://dx.doi.org/10.1037/12059-011. [8]

Nelson, C. et al. (2007), "Cognitive recovery in socially deprived young children: The Bucharest Early Intervention Project", *Science*, Vol. 318/5858, pp. 1937-1940, http://dx.doi.org/10.1126/SCIENCE.1143921. [29]

Neuenschwander, R. et al. (2012), "How do different aspects of self-regulation predict successful adaptation to school?", *Journal of Experimental Child Psychology*, Vol. 113/3, pp. 353-371, http://dx.doi.org/10.1016/J.JECP.2012.07.004. [12]

Noble, K., M. Norman and **M. Farah** (2005), "Neurocognitive correlates of socioeconomic status in kindergarten children", *Developmental Science*, Vol. 8/1, pp. 74-87, http://dx.doi.org/10.1111/j.1467-7687.2005.00394.x. [27]

Ponitz, C. et al. (2009), "A structured observation of behavioral self-regulation and its contribution to kindergarten outcomes", *Developmental Psychology*, Vol. 45/3, pp. 605-619, https://doi.org/10.1037/a0015365 (accessed on 9 July 2019). [42]

Raghubar, K., M. Barnes and **S. Hecht** (2010), "Working memory and mathematics: A review of developmental, individual difference, and cognitive approaches", *Learning and Individual Differences*, Vol. 20/2, pp. 110-122, http://dx.doi.org/10.1016/J.LINDIF.2009.10.005. [17]

Raver, C. and **C. Blair** (2016), "Neuroscientific insights: Attention, working memory, and inhibitory control", *The Future of Children*, Vol. 26/2, pp. 95-118, https://muse.jhu.edu/article/641245/summary (accessed on 27 May 2019). [37]

Raver, C., C. Blair and **M. Willoughby** (2013), "Poverty as a predictor of 4-year-olds' executive function: New perspectives on models of differential susceptibility", *Developmental Psychology*, Vol. 49/2, pp. 292-304, http://dx.doi.org/10.1037/a0028343. [28]

Schmitt, S., J. Finders and **M. McClelland** (2015), "Residential mobility, inhibitory control, and academic achievement in preschool", *Early Education and Development*, Vol. 26/2, pp. 189-208, http://dx.doi.org/10.1080/10409289.2015.975033. [36]

Shonkoff, J. and **D. Phillips** (2000), *From Neurons to Neighborhoods: The Science of Early Childhood Development*, National Acadamies Press, Washington, DC, https://www.nap.edu/catalog/9824/from-neurons-to-neighborhoods-the-science-of-early-childhood-development. [14]

Shuey, E. and **M. Kankaraš** (2018), "The Power and Promise of Early Learning", *OECD Education Working Papers*, No. 186, OECD Publishing, Paris, https://dx.doi.org/10.1787/f9b2e53f-en. [5]

Sylva, K. et al. (2003), *The effective provision of pre-school education (EPPE) project: Findings from the pre-school period*, Institute of Education, University of London, http://generic.surestart.org/pdfdir/news6.pdf (accessed on 28 February 2019). [46]

Tangney, J., R. Baumeister and **A. Boone** (2004), "High self-control predicts good adjustment, less pathology, better grades, and interpersonal success", *Journal of Personality*, Vol. 72/2, pp. 271-324, http://dx.doi.org/10.1111/j.0022-3506.2004.00263.x. [10]

Wachs, T., P. Gurkas and **S. Kontos** (2004), "Predictors of preschool children's compliance behavior in early childhood classroom settings", *Journal of Applied Developmental Psychology*, Vol. 25/4, pp. 439-457, http://dx.doi.org/10.1016/J.APPDEV.2004.06.003. [31]

Zelazo, P., C. Blair and **M. Willoughby** (2016), *Executive Function: Implications for Education (NCER 2017-2000)*, National Center for Education Research, Institute of Education Sciences, U.S. Department of Education, http://ies.ed.gov/. (accessed on 28 June 2019). [4]

Ziol-Guest, K. and **C. McKenna** (2014), "Early childhood housing instability and school readiness", *Child Development*, Vol. 85/1, pp. 103-113, http://dx.doi.org/10.1111/cdev.12105. [35]

Notes

1. Note that in each participating country, the language of assessment was the language of the ECEC centre or school the child attends. In England and the United States, the language of assessment was English and in Estonia, the assessment was carried out in Estonian or Russian.

2. Lower than 5lbs 8oz or 2.5 kg

Emergent literacy and emergent numeracy

This chapter presents findings on the emergent literacy and emergent numeracy of five-year-olds in England, Estonia and the United States. It shows how children's scores in each of these early learning domains relate to their individual characteristics, family backgrounds, home learning environments and early childhood education and care participation.

There were clear differences in children's emergent literacy and emergent numeracy across and within the three countries participating in the International Early Learning and Child Well-being Study (IELS). Children in England and Estonia had similar average scores for emergent literacy, which were higher than those in the United States. Children in England, however, had higher average scores for emergent numeracy than children in Estonia, which were in turn higher than those of children in the United States.

Within countries, differences in emergent literacy and emergent numeracy were related to the socio-economic status (SES) of children's families, the language/s spoken at home and whether children had experienced learning or behavioural difficulties. Gender clearly related to emergent literacy scores in each country, with girls' emergent literacy, on average, significantly higher than that of boys. Mothers' education levels also predicted their children's early skills, as did the nature and frequency of the activities parents undertook with their children.

The study found that children from both advantaged and disadvantaged backgrounds in the United States who had participated in early childhood education (ECEC) had higher emergent literacy and emergent numeracy scores than children who had not attended ECEC. In the United States, ECEC participation rates were higher amongst children from high socio-economic backgrounds compared to children from low socio-economic backgrounds. In England and Estonia, almost all children in the study had attended ECEC.

This chapter describes:

- the critical importance of children's early cognitive skills for their well-being and later development

- the findings of the study in relation to emergent literacy and emergent numeracy.

The findings are based on a representative sample of just under 7 000 five-year-olds in England, Estonia and the United States.

EARLY COGNITIVE SKILLS MATTER

In their early years, children's learning in different areas is inter-related and mutually reinforcing. Development in any one area supports development in related domains. For example, emergent literacy skills help children to interact well with other children. These interactions build children's prosocial skills, which in turn further strengthen their emergent literacy.

The skills children develop in early childhood are important for their immediate well-being and for their success in life. Decades of longitudinal research have shown that early literacy and numeracy are strongly predictive of later cognitive and educational outcomes (Duncan et al., 2007[1]).[1] Early literacy and numeracy skills are also associated with a range of social-emotional and economic outcomes throughout people's lives. By the time children start school, differences in their cognitive skills have already started to emerge, determined by their individual characteristics, home environments and ECEC experiences. Once these gaps exist, they become increasingly difficult and costly to close. Early intervention can address these gaps and improve the cognitive development of children in both the short and the longer term (Reynolds et al., 2002[2]; Schweinhart, 2013[3]).

Gaps in emergent literacy skills warrant early attention

Children's emergent literacy skills are a fundamental determinant of their later success in schooling and beyond, and also of their overall sense of well-being. Emergent literacy levels predict later educational achievement and attainment, employment and earnings, and overall socio-economic status. The development of children's emergent literacy skills is also linked to upward social mobility (Heckman, 2006[4]).

Emergent literacy skills also help children to communicate with others, enabling them to express themselves, understand others, and make friends. These skills are therefore integral to children's social-emotional skills and to their sense of connectedness and well-being.

The consequences of not addressing gaps in emergent literacy early on are serious. Adequate literacy levels are integral to successful functioning in most societies worldwide, yet approximately one in four (23%) 15-year-old students across OECD countries failed to reach a baseline level of proficiency[2] in reading (OECD, 2019[4]). Similarly, around one in five adults on average across OECD countries have low reading performance (OECD, 2013[5])[3]. These adults have poorer labour market outcomes and poorer self-reported health than their peers with greater proficiency in literacy. They are also more likely to feel they have little impact on the political process and are less likely to report that they trust other people (OECD, 2013[5]).

The roots of poor adult literacy are found in childhood. Children's emergent literacy skills are developed through the natural processes of learning, and through interacting with their parents, other family members and other children. As skills beget skills, children who fall behind early are likely to continue to fall further behind over time (Kautz et al., 2014[6]; Rigney, 2010[7]). Measuring children's emergent literacy skills can provide important information about where policy makers, teachers and parents could focus attention and resources in order to promote positive and equitable early literacy development and, in turn, improve children's life chances. The emergent literacy skills measured in IELS are those most closely related to and predictive of later literacy achievement, as well as other positive educational and later life outcomes.

Early numeracy is also strongly predictive of a range of later outcomes

Although emergent numeracy has been subject to less research attention than emergent literacy, longitudinal research has also identified emergent numeracy skills in early childhood as important predictors of later outcomes throughout schooling and into adulthood. Studies have shown that numeracy competence as assessed at school entry is the strongest predictor of later mathematical achievement and strongly predicts achievement in other academic domains (Duncan et al., 2007[1]). Better emergent numeracy skills in childhood are associated with higher socio-economic status in adulthood (Ritchie and Bates, 2013[8]) and with better self-reported health outcomes (OECD, 2016[9]).

On average, 24% of adults in OECD countries fail to develop numeracy skills that go beyond the ability to undertake the most basic numerical operations (OECD, 2016[9]).[4] In most countries, adults with worse information processing skills, including numeracy skills, are less likely to be employed and, when employed, tend to earn lower wages (OECD, 2016[9]). While the cost of innumeracy to individuals and societies is high now, it is likely to grow higher still in an increasingly technological and scientific world (Raghubar and Barnes, 2017[10]). Given its established importance for later outcomes, emergent numeracy was selected as an important learning domain to be assessed in IELS.

Developing a comprehensive assessment of emergent literacy and emergent numeracy

Emergent cognitive skills can be broadly categorised as either constrained or unconstrained. Constrained skills are those that are finite, such as knowing the alphabet, and these are typically easily assessed. Unconstrained skills are not limited in the same way. Unconstrained literacy skills include vocabulary knowledge and listening comprehension. Unconstrained skills develop over a longer period and are built on constrained skills (Snow and Matthews, 2016[11]). A comprehensive assessment of emergent literacy skills should assess both types of skills, and this was the approach taken in IELS. While unconstrained emergent literacy skills are generally more challenging to assess, they tend to be more strongly associated with later reading success and were therefore the primary focus of the IELS emergent literacy assessment. The assessment used innovative, play-based methods and was delivered on tablet devices.

IELS assessed three skills deemed fundamental to later literacy competence: the unconstrained skills of listening comprehension and vocabulary knowledge, and the constrained skill of phonological awareness. The direct assessment of listening comprehension in IELS had two main components: story-level listening comprehension and sentence-level listening comprehension. The former involved children listening to a story and responding to a series of audio-recorded items relating to that story, while the latter involved listening to a series of standalone sentences and responding to a single item about the meaning of each. The assessment of vocabulary knowledge in IELS required children to identify from a range of very common everyday word options ("Tier 1 words") the synonym of a more complex (Tier 2) word.[5] Finally, the phonological awareness items required children to identify the first, middle and final phonemes (sounds) of short words. IELS did not assess print knowledge, focusing instead on the early literacy and language skills that are predictive of later reading success.[6]

The general principle of focusing on the assessment of unconstrained skills in IELS was also applied to the assessment of emergent numeracy skills. The study defined emergent numeracy as the ability to recognise numbers and undertake numerical operations and reasoning in mathematics. The emphasis in the direct assessment of the children was on simple problem solving and the application of concepts and reasoning in the following content areas: numbers and counting, working with numbers, shape and space, measurement, and pattern. As with literacy, the emergent numeracy assessment was delivered on a tablet and involved children engaging with game-like activities. The emergent numeracy assessment used a mixture of drag-and-drop technology, where children moved items around the screen to construct solutions to problems, and hot-spot technology, where children tapped objects to indicate their preferred option when responding to an audio question (Figure 6.1).

The metric for all learning outcome scales in IELS is the same. There is theoretically no minimum or maximum score in IELS. The results are instead scaled to have approximately normal distributions, with the means around 500 and standard deviations around 100. The overall mean score of 500 points represents the standardised mean of all participating countries. A 1-point difference on the IELS scale therefore corresponds to an effect size of .01 of a standard deviation and a 10-point difference to an effect size of .1.

Figure 6.1 **Children were asked to "Touch who is first in line"**

OVERALL FINDINGS

Children in England and Estonia have stronger emergent literacy than children in the United States, while children in England have stronger emergent numeracy than children in the other two countries

There were clear differences in children's emergent literacy as assessed in IELS within and across the three countries participating in the study. Table 6.1 sets out the mean scores from the direct assessments of children's emergent literacy and emergent numeracy in England, Estonia and the United States, with the distributions shown in Figure 6.2.

Table 6.1 **Mean emergent literacy and numeracy scores, by country**

	Mean emergent literacy score	Mean emergent numeracy score
Estonia	508	500
England	515	529
United States	477	471

StatLink https://doi.org/10.1787/888934111246

Children in England had the highest average emergent literacy score across the three countries, although the mean score in England was not significantly different from that in Estonia. The United States had the narrowest distribution of scores for emergent literacy, with a smaller percentage of children at the highest levels and a relatively larger proportion at the lowest levels than in the other countries. Estonia's results lie between those of the other two countries, although more closely resemble England's profile than that of the United States.

Children in England had higher average emergent numeracy than children in the other two countries. England also had the largest proportion of children with the highest levels of emergent numeracy. Estonia's results on emergent numeracy sit between those of England and the United States. The mean score for emergent numeracy in the United States was well below the means of the other two countries, with the United States having fewer children than the other two countries who demonstrated high levels of emergent numeracy.

Children's emergent literacy and emergent numeracy increase with age

Children develop and learn quickly during their early years. The differences in scores by age give an estimate of expected learning progressions. Figure 6.3 sets out the mean emergent literacy and emergent numeracy scores of children in England, Estonia and the United States by their ages in months.

Figure 6.2 **Distribution of emergent literacy and emergent numeracy scores by country**

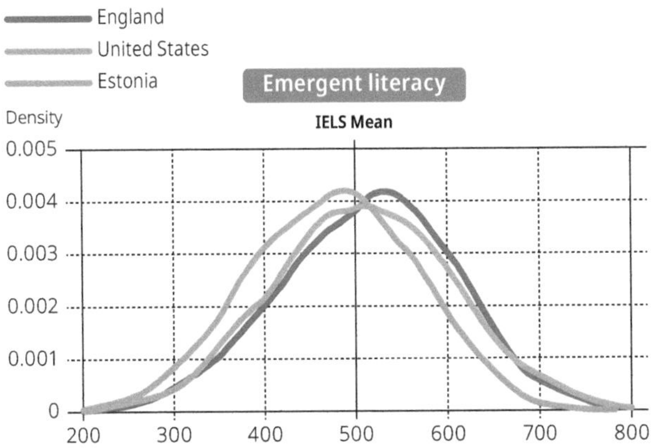

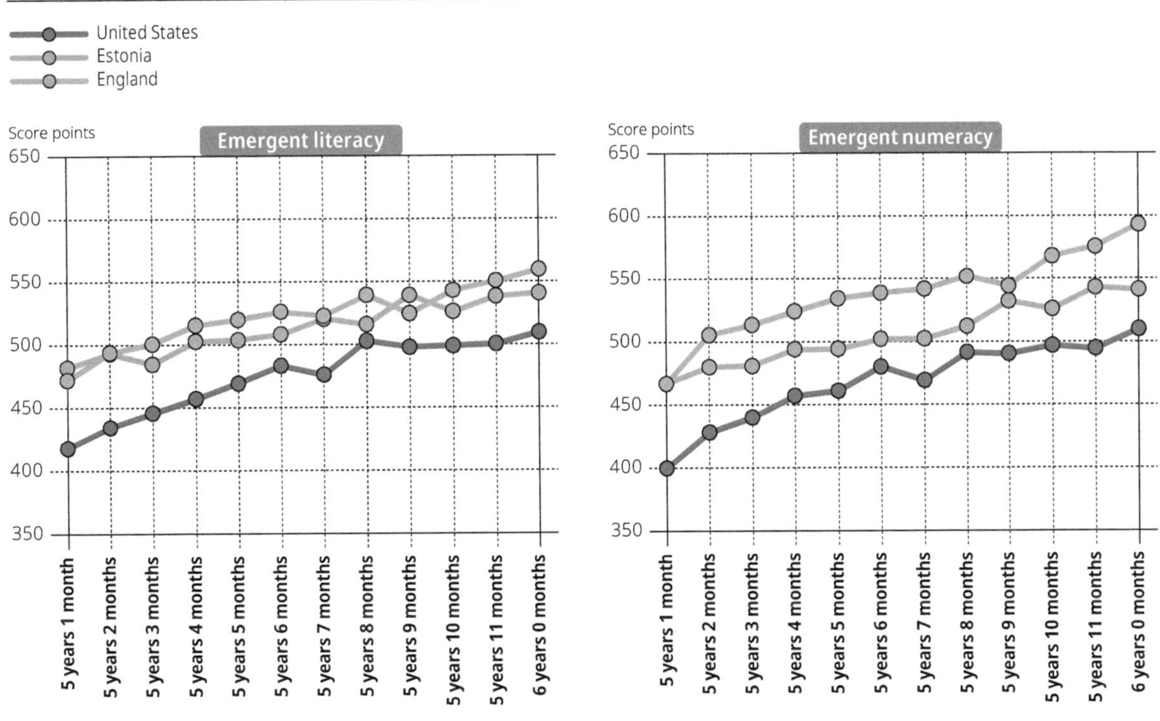

For emergent literacy, scores for the youngest children in the United States were lower than in the other countries, rapidly increased with age up to 5 years, 6 months, then levelled off among the older children in the group. The gradient among children in the United States in this second 6-month age group was similar to that among children in England and Estonia. However, the gap between children in the United States and children in England and Estonia had not closed among the six-year-olds.

In emergent numeracy, the indicative rate of progress across age in months was broadly similar across the three countries, although it was slightly lower in Estonia.

The average increase in emergent literacy scores for each month of age was 8 points in the United States, 8 points in England and 5 points in Estonia. The corresponding averages for emergent numeracy are were 10 points in the United States, 11 points for England and 7 points for Estonia. The strength of the relationship between age and learning was similar in all SES quartiles and for boys and girls, in both domains.

Figure 6.3 **Emergent literacy and emergent numeracy scores by age of child in months by country**

In addition to directly assessing children's emergent literacy and emergent numeracy, parents and teachers were also asked to rate each child's expressive language development (defined as the degree to which the child uses language effectively, can communicate ideas, etc), receptive language development (the extent to which the child understands, interprets and listens), and numeracy development, relative to other five-year-olds. Figure 6.4 sets out the mean percentages of children rated as below average, average or above average in each domain by their parents and teachers across the three participating countries.

The indirect assessments of children's literacy and numeracy by parents and teachers were broadly aligned with the results of the direct assessments, i.e. children who were reported to have above average development in these areas by their parents and teachers had higher average scores on the direct assessments than other children.

Parents rated their children's emergent literacy and emergent numeracy more highly than teachers in all three countries. There may be many reasons for this. For example, children can behave differently at home than at their ECEC centre or school. At the same time, teachers have knowledge of a wider group of children than parents to inform their assessment of each child.

Figure 6.4 **Receptive language, expressive language and numeracy development as reported by parents and teachers**

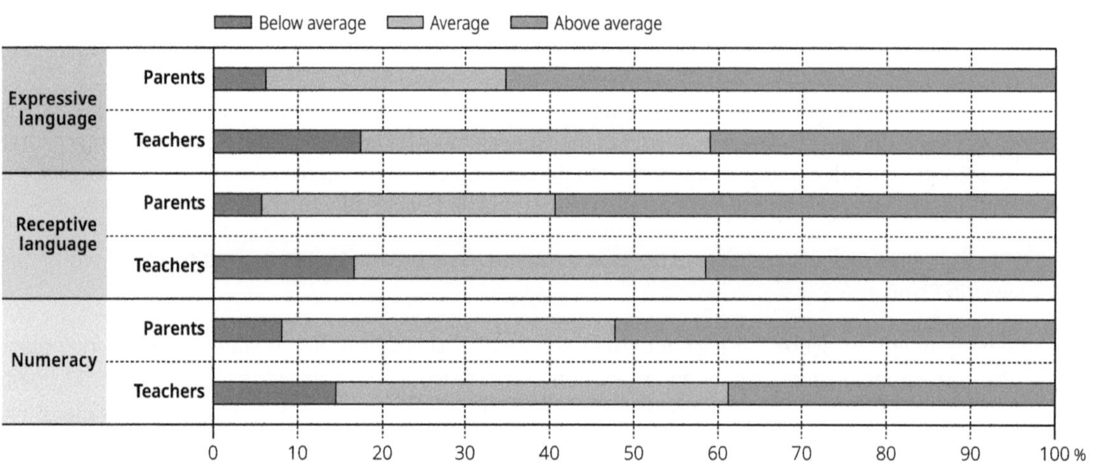

StatLink https://doi.org/10.1787/888934110942

There were many similarities across the three countries in the factors associated with higher and lower levels of emergent literacy and emergent numeracy, discussed in the following sections.

Girls do better in emergent literacy but the same as boys in numeracy

Girls in all three countries demonstrated higher average emergent literacy than boys (Figure 6.5). These findings are consistent with other international studies of children's literacy, albeit at older ages, such as the Progress in International Reading Literacy Study[7]. The size of the gender difference in emergent literacy was similar in all three countries.

Figure 6.5 **Emergent literacy scores by gender**

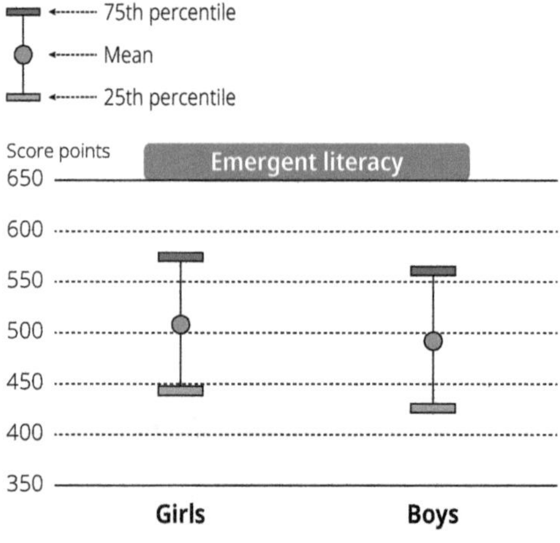

Note: The gender differences at the 25th percentile, the mean and the 75th percentile are statistically significant.

StatLink https://doi.org/10.1787/888934110961

There were no significant gender differences in emergent numeracy in any of the three participating countries at age five. This stands in contrast to the findings of several large-scale assessments of the mathematics achievement of older children and students (e.g. in PISA), where differences in favour of boys are found in many countries.

The reports from parents and from teachers on the children's literacy development also identified clear gender gaps in both expressive and receptive language development, as well as gender gaps in numeracy (shown in Figure 6.6).

As Figure 6.6 shows, girls were more likely than boys to be considered to have above-average numeracy development, and this was most pronounced in the teachers' assessments. This is in contrast with the direct assessment of children's emergent numeracy, which found no significant differences between girls and boys at the mean, at the 25th percentile or at the 75th percentile.

Figure 6.6 **Expressive language, receptive language and numeracy development as reported by parents and teachers, by gender**

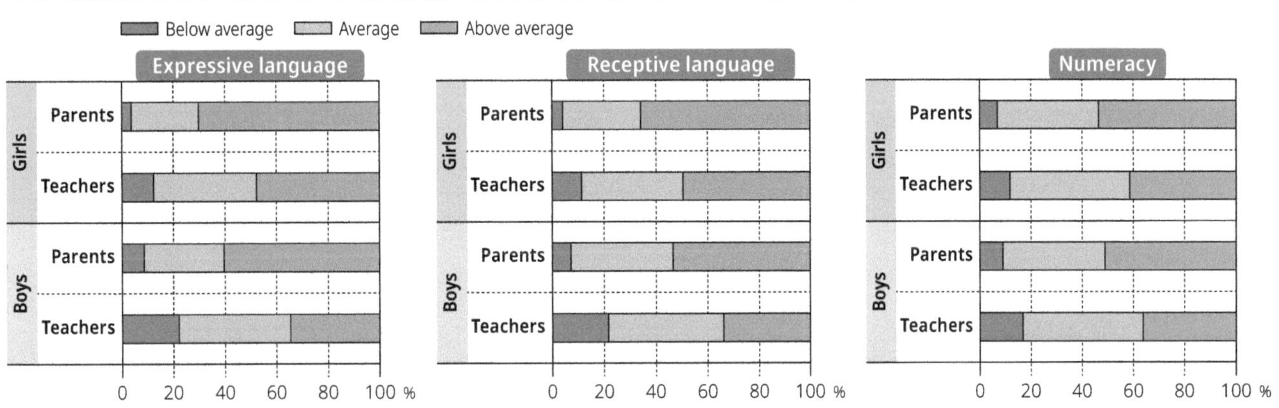

StatLink ＝ https://doi.org/10.1787/888934110980

Socio-economic status is less strongly related to children's learning in Estonia than in England or the United States

Many studies have found that the socio-economic status of children's families is associated with their learning outcomes. The extent to which children's backgrounds are associated with their education outcomes varies widely across countries, with some education systems more successful in mitigating disadvantage than others. By understanding which countries do this best and how, policy makers and education leaders can learn from these experiences, set expectations and put strategies in place to achieve more equitable outcomes for children.

The emergent literacy and emergent numeracy scores of the children taking part in IELS were significantly associated with their socio-economic background, as Figure 6.7 shows. The relationship between learning and SES was similar for girls and boys, for both emergent literacy and emergent numeracy.

Figure 6.7 **Emergent literacy and emergent numeracy scores by socio-economic quartile**

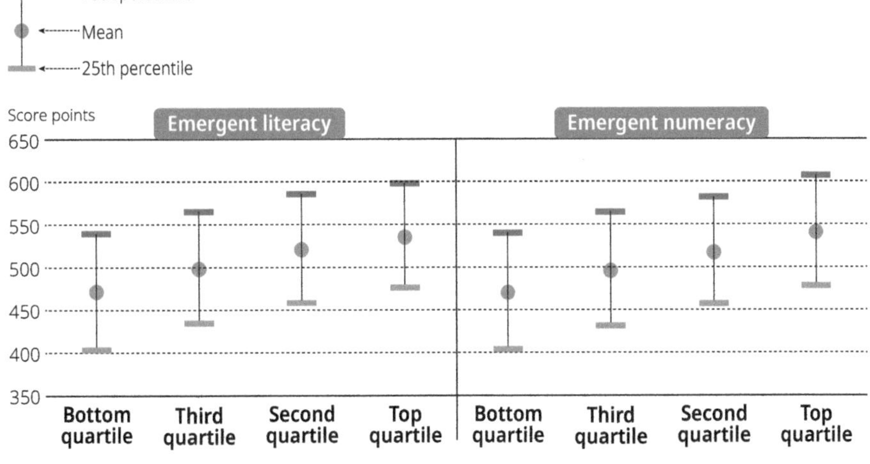

StatLink ＝ https://doi.org/10.1787/888934110999

Children in Estonia had the smallest differences in both emergent literacy and emergent numeracy scores across the socio-economic quartiles. This is consistent with findings in the Programme for International Student Assessment (PISA), where Estonia achieved greater equity in outcomes than England or the United States. The relationship between SES and children's learning was similar in England and the United States for emergent literacy, whereas the association between SES and emergent numeracy was stronger in the United States than in England.

Reports from parents and teachers for both emergent literacy and emergent numeracy were generally aligned with the findings from the direct assessments. Thus, although parents and teachers tended to rate some children more highly than their direct assessment scores suggested, the different levels of development of children in each socio-economic quartile indicated by the direct assessment were discernible by both parents and teachers.

Figure 6.8 **Emergent literacy and emergent numeracy development as reported by parents and teachers by socio-economic quartile**

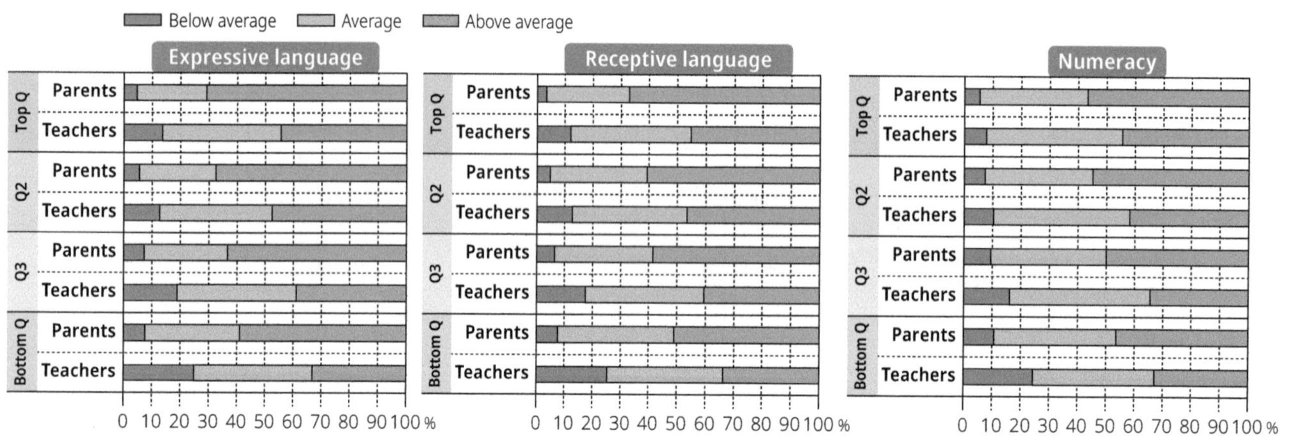

StatLink https://doi.org/10.1787/888934111018

There were no differences between children based solely on their immigration background

The study found no significant differences in overall scores for children from families with an immigrant background, once socio-economic status and home language were taken into account. An immigrant background is defined in IELS has having both parents born in a different country.[8] Across the three countries, on average 12% of children had an immigrant background.

At the individual country level, however, there were small significant differences for children with an immigrant background in England. Children in England from families with a migrant background had lower emergent literacy scores than those from non-immigrant backgrounds, even after adjusting for SES and home language. No such differences were found in the United States or in Estonia.

Home language is associated with children's emergent literacy and emergent numeracy

The parents of children in the study were also asked to indicate whether one or both of the child's parents spoke a language at home that is different from the language of the ECEC centre or school that the child attends. On average, 13% of children across the three countries had a different home language: 20% of children in the United States, 16% in England and 6% in Estonia.

The direct assessments were carried out in English in England and in the United States, and in Estonian or Russian in Estonia. Having a home language that is different from the assessment language was negatively associated with emergent literacy scores and numeracy scores, as shown in Figure 6.9. This was true in all three participating countries.

Children with a home language different to the assessment language were also more likely to be rated as having below average language and numeracy development by their parents and teachers than other children (Figure 6.10). The gap between parents' and teachers' ratings were wider for children with a different home language than for other children.

Figure 6.9 **Children's emergent literacy and numeracy scores, by home language**

Score-point differences between children who have at least one parent at home who speaks mainly a language different to the assessment language and those who do not, before and after accounting for socio-economic status

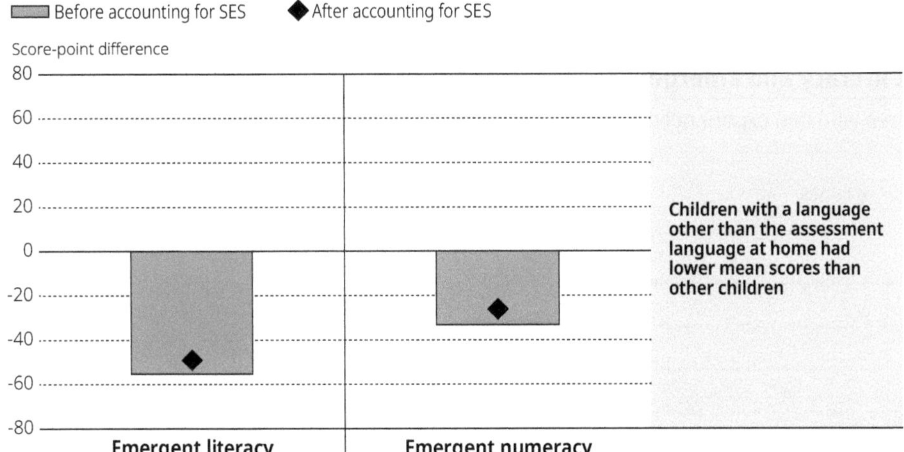

Note: All differences are statistically significant.
StatLink https://doi.org/10.1787/888934111037

Figure 6.10 **Emergent literacy and emergent numeracy as reported by parents and teachers by home language, combined results**

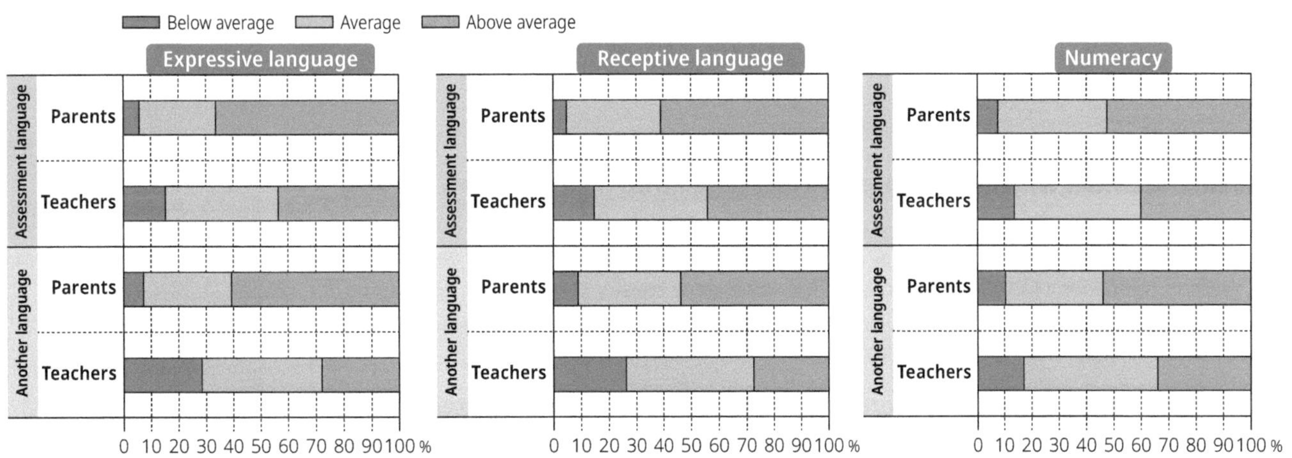

StatLink https://doi.org/10.1787/888934111056

Children with learning or behavioural difficulties have lower emergent literacy and numeracy

Parents were also asked whether their child had a low birth weight[9] or was born prematurely, had learning difficulties (e.g. speech or language delay, intellectual disability) or social, emotional or behavioural difficulties. On average across countries, 24% of children had experienced at least one of these challenges. An average of 9% of children were reported to have had low birth weight or have been premature, 11% had experienced learning difficulties and 10% had social, emotional or behavioural difficulties.

Overall, parents in England and Estonia reported slightly fewer children with these challenges than parents in the United States. Estonian parents reported the smallest proportion of children who had low birth weight or who were premature, while parents in England reported the smallest proportion of children with behavioural difficulties.

There was no significant gender difference in the proportion of children who had a low birth weight or were premature. Boys were twice as likely as girls to be reported by their parents as having experienced learning difficulties and also significantly more likely than girls to be reported by their parents as having social, emotional or behavioural difficulties.

Children with learning difficulties and children with social, emotional or behavioural difficulties had lower mean scores in both emergent literacy and emergent numeracy than children without these difficulties, after accounting for SES. Additionally, after accounting for socio-economic status, children who had had a low birth weight or were premature had a significantly lower mean emergent numeracy score than other children, but there was no corresponding association with emergent literacy in any of the three participating countries. The score-point differences between children with and without these challenges are shown in Figure 6.11 below.

Figure 6.11 **Children's emergent literacy and emergent numeracy, by early learning challenges**

Score-point differences between children who had experienced an early difficulty and those who had not, before and after accounting for socio-economic status

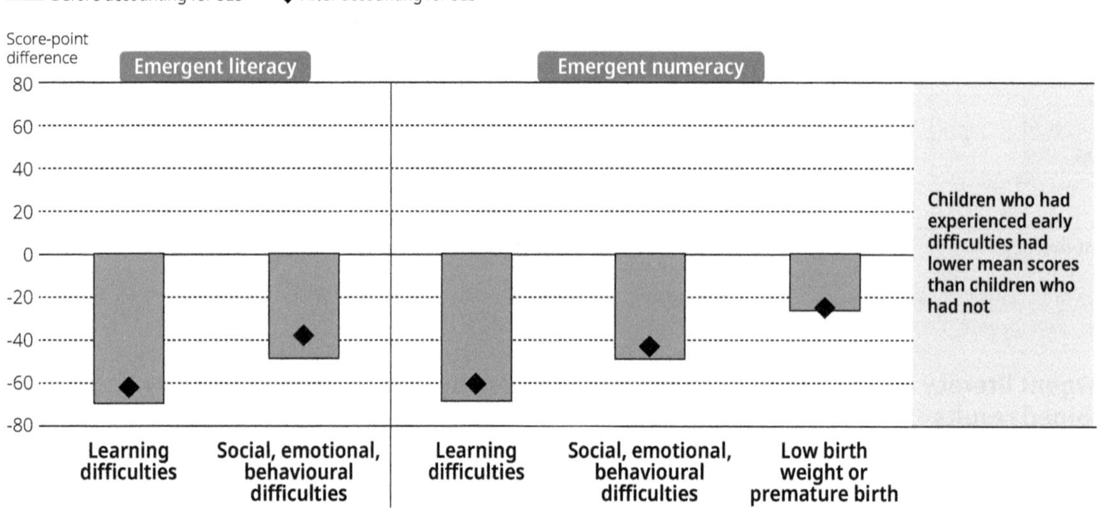

Note: All differences are statistically significant.

StatLink https://doi.org/10.1787/888934111075

Parents' activities with their children are associated with their children's learning

The activities parents undertake with their children are significantly related to their children's learning. In this study, parents were asked whether and how often they read to their children from books. There were positive associations between frequency of reading to children from books and children's emergent literacy scores, after accounting for SES, as shown in Figure 6.12. Children who were read to on at least five days each week had the highest mean scores. Parents reported that they read with their daughters as much as with their sons.

Figure 6.12 **Emergent literacy scores by engagement in literacy-related activities at home**

Score-point differences between children whose parents read to them at home on at least one day a week and those whose parents do so less often, before and after accounting for socio-economic status

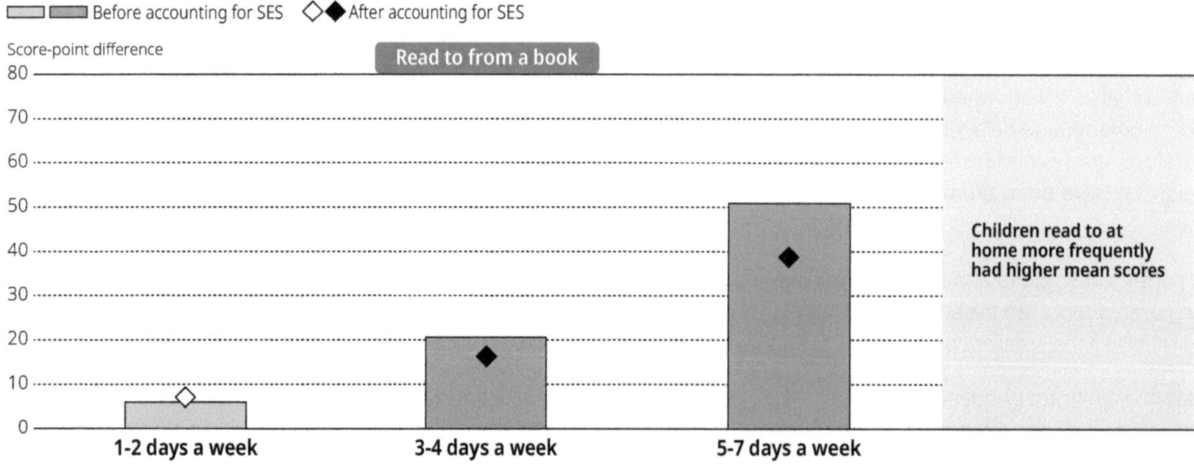

Note: Statistically significant differences are shown in a darker tone.

StatLink https://doi.org/10.1787/888934111094

 | **© OECD 2020** Early Learning and Child Well-being: A Study of five-year-olds in England, Estonia and the United States

A higher proportion of parents in England (59%) reported that they read to their children 5-7 days a week than parents in Estonia (38%) or the United States (43%). Children from advantaged backgrounds were much more likely to be read to 5-7 days a week (60% on average across the three countries) than children from disadvantaged backgrounds (30%).

The study also found that the number of children's books in children's homes was positively associated with both emergent literacy and emergent numeracy scores, after accounting for socio-economic status (Figure 6.13). Children in England were more likely to live in homes with more than 100 children's books than children in the other two countries. Across all three countries, children from high SES backgrounds were twice as likely to have more than 100 children's books in their homes than children from low SES backgrounds.

Figure 6.13 **Emergent literacy and emergent numeracy scores by number of children's books in the home**

Score-point differences between children with more children's books at home and those with ten books or fewer, before and after accounting for socio-economic status

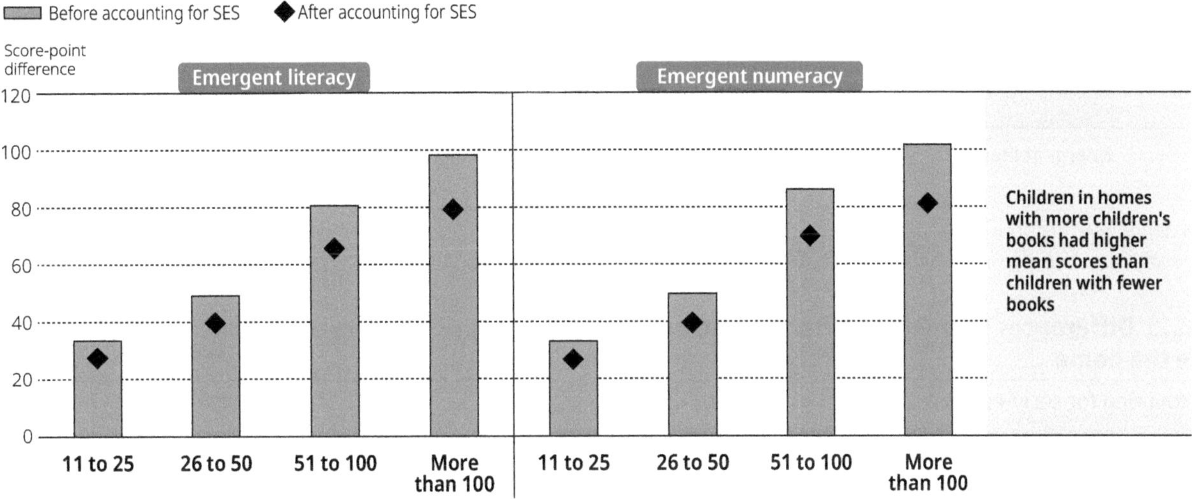

Note: All differences are statistically significant.
StatLink https://doi.org/10.1787/888934111113

A further factor that was positively associated with children's emergent literacy and emergent numeracy development was the extent to which their parents were involved in their ECEC centre or school (Figure 6.14). Teachers were asked how involved parents were with the ECEC centre or school the child attended, ranging from not involved to slightly, moderately or strongly involved. Teachers in Estonia reported that 80% of parents were moderately or strongly involved, compared to 69% of parents in England and 65% in the United States. Children whose parents were rated as more strongly involved had higher mean emergent literacy and emergent numeracy scores than other children, regardless of socio-economic status. More parents from high SES groups (84%) were reported to be involved in their child's ECEC centre or school than parents from low SES groups (67%). Parents were as likely to be involved in the ECEC centre or school of their son as that of their daughter.

Taking children to special activities outside the home, such as sports or scouts, was also positively associated with emergent literacy and emergent numeracy development, as shown in Figure 6.15. Overall, children who attend special activities had higher mean scores in emergent literacy and emergent numeracy than those who did not, after accounting for socio-economic status.

Children in Estonia were more likely to attend special activities at least 3 times a week (25%) than children in England (18%) or the United States (18%), whereas children in the United States were more likely to never attend or attend less than once a week (46%) than children in the other two countries (36% in Estonia and 35% in England). Boys and girls were, on average, equally likely to be taken to such activities. Children from low socio-economic backgrounds were more likely to never attend such activities or do so less than once a week (56% on average across the three countries), compared to children from high socio-economic backgrounds (26%).

Figure 6.14 **Emergent literacy and emergent numeracy scores by level of parental involvement in children's ECEC centres or schools**

Score-point differences between children whose parents are moderately or strongly involved and those who are slightly or not involved, before and after accounting for socio-economic status

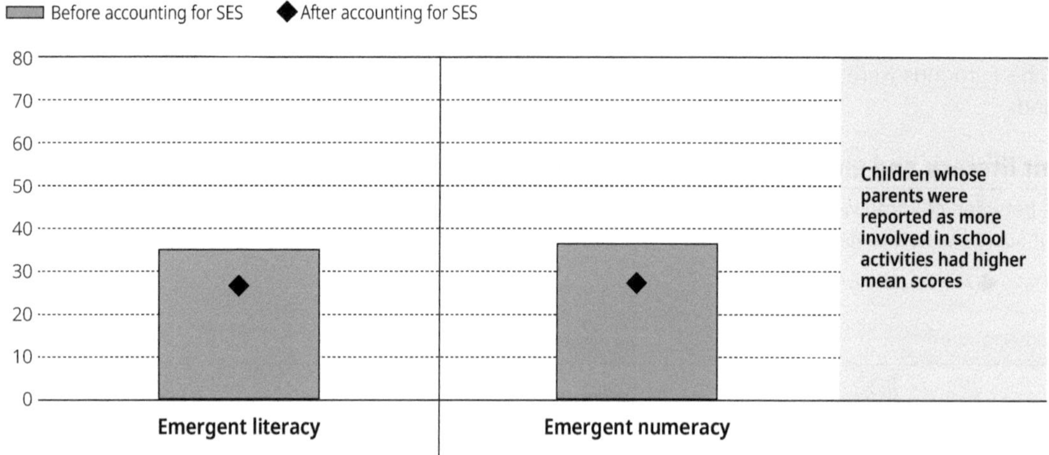

Note: All differences are statistically significant.

StatLink https://doi.org/10.1787/888934111132

Figure 6.15 **Differences in emergent literacy and numeracy scores by engagement in special activities outside the home**

After accounting for socio-economic status

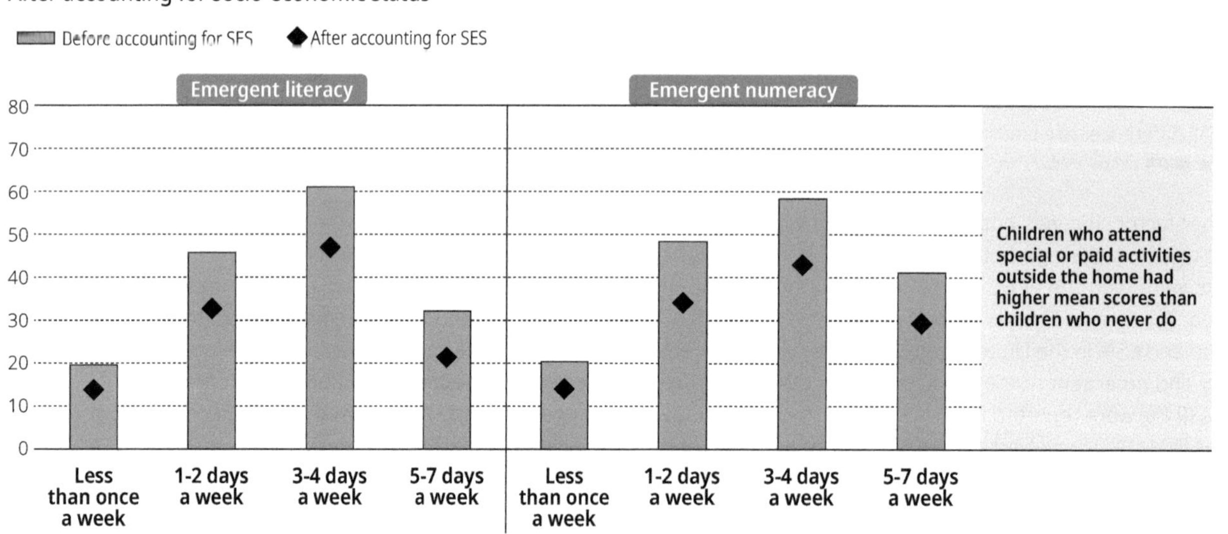

Note: All differences are statistically significant.

StatLink https://doi.org/10.1787/888934111151

Mothers' education levels are positively associated with their children's learning

Parents with higher levels of education are more likely to engage their children in activities that help them to learn, such as reading from books (Sylva et al., 2008[14]). Studies on children's early development have also found independent positive effects from mothers' education in particular.

As noted in Chapter 3, the mothers of the children in Estonia in the study were more likely to have a bachelor's degree (53%) than in either England (40%) or the United States (39%). The mean emergent literacy and numeracy scores of children across all three countries were significantly higher for children whose mothers had at least a bachelor's degree (Figure 6.16).

Figure 6.16 **Emergent literacy and emergent numeracy scores by mothers' educational attainment**

Score-point differences between children whose mothers held bachelor's degrees and those whose mothers did not, before and after accounting for socio-economic status

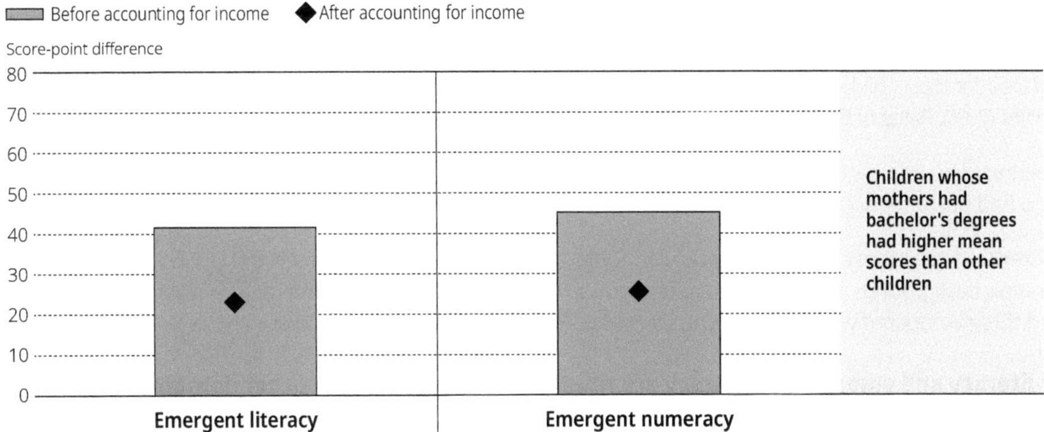

Note: All differences are statistically significant.

StatLink https://doi.org/10.1787/888934111170

The use of digital devices had little overall significant associations with children's emergent literacy or emergent numeracy

On average, 83% of children across the three participating countries used a digital device at least once a week, with 42% using one every day. Only 7% of children on average never or hardly ever used such devices, with 10% using one at least monthly, but not weekly.

Overall, children who never used digital devices had mean scores that did not differ greatly from those of children who did use them, after accounting for socio-economic status. In the United States, however, there were some positive associations between emergent literacy and using a digital device at least monthly or weekly, but not daily. In England, there was a positive association with emergent literacy and using a device monthly, but not weekly or daily.

Children from single-parent households do as well in emergent literacy as those from two-parent households, but less well on numeracy

On average across the three participating countries, 86% of the children in the study lived in two-parent households. There were no significant differences in emergent literacy between children in single-parent households and other children after accounting for socio-economic status. However, the emergent numeracy scores of children in single-parent households were lower, once SES was accounted for (Fig 6.17).

Figure 6.17 **Emergent numeracy scores by household structure**

Score-point differences between children in single-parent households and two-parent households, before and after accounting for socio-economic status

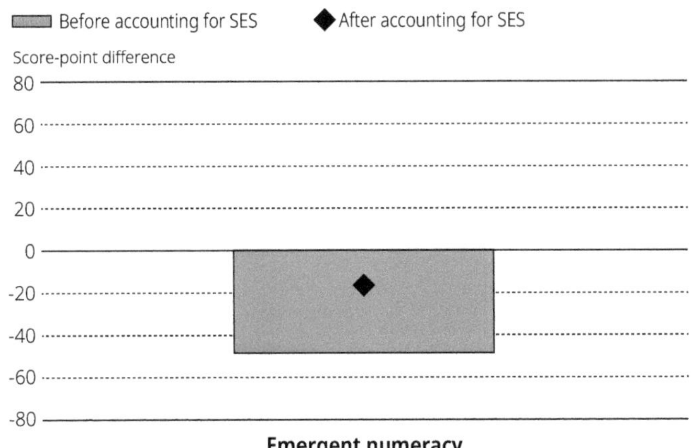

Note: All differences are statistically significant.

StatLink https://doi.org/10.1787/888934111189

System-wide provision of ECEC may provide benefits for children

In England and Estonia, almost all children attend ECEC, including children from disadvantaged backgrounds. In the United States, however, this is not the case. In 2017, 100% of three-year-olds in the United Kingdom participated in ECEC, compared to 91% in Estonia and 42% in the United States, against an OECD average of 79% (OECD, 2019[4]).

In the United States, ECEC participation rates among the children taking part in IELS varied significantly depending on the socio-economic status of their families. Children from advantaged families were more likely (91%) to have attended ECEC than children from disadvantaged families (73%). Rates of ECEC attendance did not vary significantly across different ethnic and racial groups.

In the United States, children who had participated in ECEC had significantly higher emergent literacy and emergent numeracy scores than children who had not, after accounting for SES. These differences were particularly strong for emergent numeracy.

The study found no differences in children's emergent literacy or numeracy based on the age they started ECEC. After accounting for children's socio-economic backgrounds, there were no differences in emergent literacy and numeracy for children who started ECEC before they turned three compared with children who started ECEC as three-year-olds or older.

Children's emergent literacy and emergent numeracy are related to their learning in other domains

In the early years, children's learning is inter-related and mutually reinforcing. Development in any one area supports development in related domains. For the five-year-olds in this study, there was a large amount of overlap between emergent literacy and emergent numeracy skills and the other domains assessed in IELS, as shown in Figure 6.18 and Figure 6.19.

Figure 6.18 **Correlations between emergent literacy scores and other learning domains**

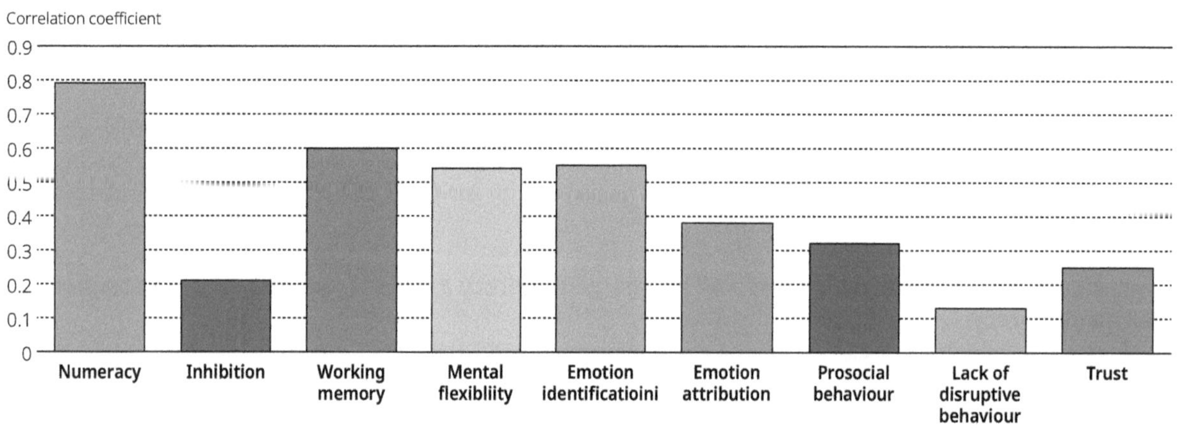

Note: All correlations are statistically significant.

StatLink https://doi.org/10.1787/888934111208

Figure 6.19 **Correlations between emergent numeracy scores and other learning domains,**

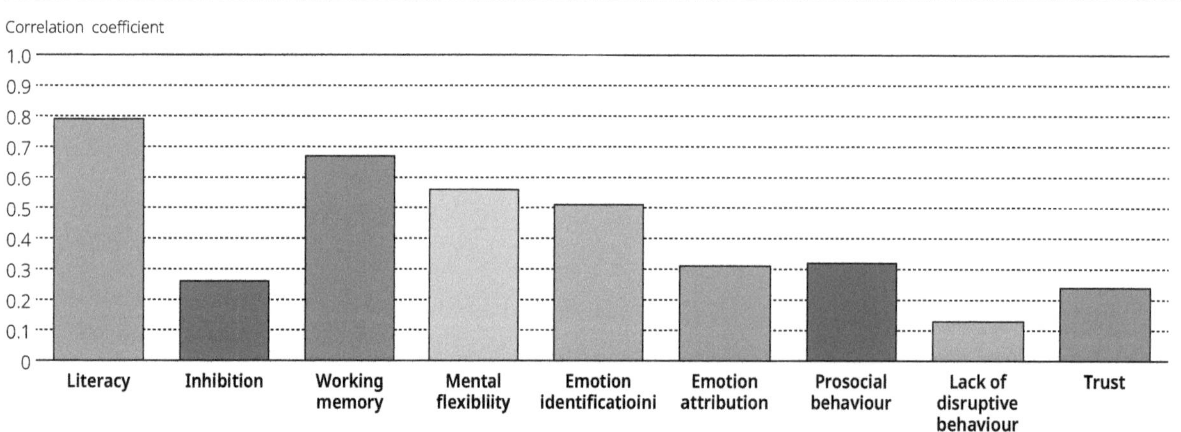

Note: All correlations are statistically significant.

StatLink https://doi.org/10.1787/888934111227

The correlations between emergent literacy scores and other early learning domains were similar for England, Estonia and the United States. They were also similar for girls and for boys, and across socio-economic groups.

Generally, the strength of the relationships between emergent literacy and other learning domains and between emergent numeracy and other learning domains were similar. Again, the strength of the correlations between early numeracy and other early learning domains was similar across countries, between girls and boys, and across socio-economic groups.

CONCLUSIONS

Children in England and Estonia had similar mean scores for emergent literacy, which were higher than those in the United States. Children in England, however, had higher scores for emergent numeracy than children in Estonia, which in turn were higher than those of children in the United States.

In all three countries, girls' emergent literacy was more advanced than that of boys, both in the direct assessment and in the ratings provided by parents and teachers. There were no significant gender differences, however, in the findings from the direct assessment of emergent numeracy. Nonetheless, parents and teachers both rated girls as having higher levels of numeracy than boys.

The study found a clear relationship between children's early learning and the socio-economic status of the child's family. This relationship was strongest in the United States and least pronounced in Estonia.

Another factor negatively associated with children's emergent literacy and emergent numeracy scores was having a home language different from the language of the ECEC centre or school that the child attended. This suggests that supporting these children's skills in the language of the school or centre, while also supporting their home language, is and will continue to be important for their development.

While coming from a single-parent or two-parent household did not have a large relationship with children's learning, having a well-educated mother did. However, the activities parents undertook with their children clearly supported early cognitive development, even amongst parents with little formal education. Key activities that parents undertake that are associated with stronger cognitive development include:

- reading to their children from books on at least 5-7 days a week

- being involved in the child's ECEC centre or school

- providing children's books in the home

- taking to children to special activities.

While the provision of ECEC is system-wide in both England and Estonia, this is not the case in the United States. Yet children in the United States who had participated in ECEC had significantly higher emergent literacy and emergent numeracy scores than children who had not attended ECEC, after accounting for socio-economic status. These differences were particularly strong in emergent numeracy.

At an aggregate level across the three countries, children's use of digital devices was not significantly associated with their emergent literacy or emergent numeracy skills.

References

Beck, I., M. McKeown and **L. Kucan** (2013), *Bringing words to life : robust vocabulary instruction*, The Guilford Press. [13]

Duncan, G. et al. (2007), "School readiness and later achievement", *Psychological Association*, Vol. 43/6, pp. 1428-1446, http://dx.doi.org/10.1037/[0012-1649.43.6.1428].supp. [1]

Kautz, T. et al. (2014), "Fostering and measuring skills: Improving cognitive and non-cognitive skills to promote lifetime success", *NBER Working Paper Series*, No. 20749, National Bureau of Economic Research, Cambridge, MA, http://dx.doi.org/10.3386/w20749. [6]

OECD (2019), *PISA 2018 Results (Volume I): What Students Know and Can Do*, PISA, OECD Publishing, Paris, https://dx.doi.org/10.1787/5f07c754-en. [4]

OECD (2016), *Skills Matter: Further Results from the Survey of Adult Skills*, OECD Skills Studies, OECD Publishing, Paris, https://dx.doi.org/10.1787/9789264258051-en. [9]

OECD (2013), *OECD Skills Outlook 2013: First Results from the Survey of Adult Skills*, OECD Publishing, Paris, https://dx.doi.org/10.1787/9789264204256-en. [5]

Raghubar, K. and **M. Barnes** (2017), "Early numeracy skills in preschool-aged children: A review of neurocognitive findings and implications for assessment and intervention", *Clinical Neuropsychology*, Vol. 31/2, pp. 329-351, http://dx.doi.org/10.1080/13854046.2016.1259387. [10]

Reynolds, A. et al. (2002), "Age 21 cost-benefit analysis of the Title I Chicago Child-Parent Centers", *Educational Evaluation and Policy Analysis*, Vol. 24/4, pp. 267-303, http://dx.doi.org/10.3102/01623737024004267. [2]

Rigney, D. (2010), *The Matthew Effect: How Advantage Begets Further Advantage*, Columbia University Press. [7]

Ritchie, S. and **T. Bates** (2013), "Enduring links from childhood mathematics and reading achievement to adult socioeconomic status", *Psychological Science*, Vol. 24/7, pp. 1301-1308, http://dx.doi.org/10.1177/0956797612466268. [8]

Schweinhart, L. (2013), "Long-term follow-up of a preschool experiment", *Journal of Experimental Criminology*, Vol. 9/4, pp. 389-409, http://dx.doi.org/10.1007/s11292-013-9190-3. [3]

Shuey, E. and **M. Kankaraš** (2018), "The Power and Promise of Early Learning", *OECD Education Working Papers*, No. 186, OECD Publishing, Paris, https://dx.doi.org/10.1787/f9b2e53f-en. [12]

Snow, C. and **T. Matthews** (2016), *Reading and Language in the Early Grades*, http://www.futureofchildren.org (accessed on 5 December 2019). [11]

Sylva, K. et al. (2008), *Final report from the primary phase: Pre-school, school and family influences on children's development during Key Stage 2 (7-11) Publication Details*, http://ro.uow.edu.au/sspapers/1807 (accessed on 4 February 2020). [14]

Notes

1. For a fuller description of relevant longitudinal studies refer to Shuey and Kankaraš (2018[13]).

2. Scoring at or below Proficiency Level 1 in PISA Reading.

3. Scoring at or below Proficiency Level 1 in PIAAC Reading.

4. Scoring at or below Proficiency Level 1 in PIAAC Numeracy.

5. Beck, McKeown and Kucan (2013[13]) propose a three-tier model of vocabulary development, where Tier 1 words are common words used in everyday speech (e.g. table, blue), Tier 2 words are high-frequency words that occur across contexts and are more common in written than spoken language (e.g. compare, coincidence). Tier 3 words are low-frequency words used in domain-specific contexts (e.g. thesis, ecosystem).

6. For more information, see the IELS assessment framework.

7. For further information see: https://www.iea.nl/studies/iea/pirls

8. Or one parent, where information was only available for one parent.

9. Lower than 5lbs 8 oz or 2.5 kg

ANNEX A

Technical note

This technical note provides additional background information on technical aspects relating to the International Early Learning the Child Well-being Study (IELS). It sets out the rationale for the types of assessment used in the study, response rates and other factors influencing the robustness, reliability and comparability of the data. More information on the conceptual and technical aspects of the study can be found in the Assessment Framework and Technical Standards for the study.

Assessment methods

The study used two types of assessment: direct assessment of children's skills through developmentally-appropriate, interactive stories and games delivered on a tablet device and indirect assessment through reports on children's skills from parents and teachers. The key benefit of direct assessment is that it provides countries with a common basis for comparing children's early learning. Through careful development, testing and analysis[1], any cultural or other biases are minimised so that countries can have confidence that the results are comparable across countries. Furthermore, delivery of the assessment through a tablet device enhances the reliability of the results through the avoidance of transcription and coding errors.

The indirect assessment provides benefits in triangulating the results from the direct assessment and in providing a fuller picture of children's development and skills. Parents have knowledge of their child over time and in a range of settings, whereas teachers have a comparative group of children at the same age on which to base their assessments. Thus, gaining information from parents as well as from teachers provides greater breadth and depth on children's early learning and development while the direct assessment provides a stronger basis for comparability across countries.

Participation rates

A critical factor influencing the reliability of the results from any survey is the response rates, particularly for any form of direct assessment. The quality standard for child participation rates for IELS was set at 75%, meaning this level of participation rate provides confidence that the sample is representative of children at that age in that country. Each participating country exceeded this standard. Teacher response rates were also very high, 90% or higher in each country. While parent response rates were somewhat lower, these were still higher than is generally expected.

Table A.1 **Response rates for IELS, by informant and country**

Participation rates	England (%)	Estonia (%)	United States (%)
Child	94.9	84.1	92.7
Parent	67.5	86.0	71.2
Teacher	89.7	94.1	96.4

Note: The participation rates are weighted and based on participating centre/schools and children.

Quality assurance

Standards for administration and assessment procedures, to achieve standardised implementation procedures, were set out in comprehensive manuals, applicable to each participating country. Precise instructions were provided for centre and school co-ordinators and scripts were provided to study administrators, in addition to the provision of mandatory training.

National and International Quality Assurance Monitors (IQAMs) were appointed to attest that the implementation in each country complied with the standards for the study. These Quality Monitors were independent and observed the administration of the assessments in each participating country in order to attest that the required standards were met. Across all quality assurance activities, the observations showed that all three participating countries generally followed the standardized procedures as outlined in the IELS Technical Standards.

Note

1. The types of analysis used for this study included differential item functioning by gender, country, and language, item-level analysis, latent trait-level analysis, and convergent and predictive validity analysis.

Printed by Libri Plureos GmbH in Hamburg,
Germany